Follow the Way

Follow the Way

Listen. Be. See.

LARS COBURN

Foreword by Janel Coburn

RESOURCE *Publications* · Eugene, Oregon

FOLLOW THE WAY
Listen. Be. See.

Resource Publications
An Imprint of Wipf and Stock Publishers
199 W. 8th Ave., Suite 3
Eugene, OR 97401

www.wipfandstock.com

PAPERBACK ISBN: 978-1-5326-5975-1
HARDCOVER ISBN: 978-1-5326-5976-8
EBOOK ISBN: 978-1-5326-5977-5

Manufactured in the U.S.A.   02/29/20

For my daughter Ashlynn Selah Coburn, may you grow up in a home filled with humility, gratitude, and simplicity. Thank you for teaching me so much about God.

Contents

Foreword

As I've watched my husband labor over this book for the last few years, I have marveled at the motivation that flowed through him. He sat for countless hours to get his words on these pages and we've had hundreds of conversations revolving around what you're about to read. His love for you, unknown reader, is greater than you could ever imagine. He's poured over these thoughts to make them the best versions of themselves so they would make the most sense for you. If you're a lay-person like me, don't worry! I have read and re-read this book more times than I can count, and every time I've made edits and suggestions that leave this book more accessible to you. (And if you're a sucker for geek speak like my dear husband, you'll be overjoyed to see the five syllable words and quotes from big shots scattered among the writing as well.)

Lars' passion and insight are so strongly shown in the pages to come, you can't help but fall more in love with Jesus because of it. As I've read these words over and over again, I've been hit repeatedly by the importance of the three virtues outlined. In self reflection now, I can honestly say I have learned vital lessons in humility, simplicity, and gratitude through the conversations we've had as a couple that have shaped this writing. Our daughter is better off because we were brave enough to engage in the tough conversations and endeavor in becoming people that emulate these virtues. My greatest hope is that she'll grow up watching us live our lives in a never ending cycle of learning and adapting. I have gained perspective, knowledge, and insight into the scriptures through these pages and I can only pray the same will be true for you.

Please know that as you flip through these pages, you have prayer warriors behind you that are pleading with God to open your eyes to the ways in which you can grow closer to Him. With that, dear reader, may God's richest blessings be over you as you work through this literature.

JANEL COBURN

Preface

Knowing God through Humility, Gratitude, & Simplicity

My dream is that a variety of people will pick up this book and find useful nuggets throughout it. I have written this to be a resource for scholars, ministers, church goers, new faith-ers, and no faith-ers alike! I've intentionally integrated pieces of my academic learning from my time in seminary with my real life experiences to make the information included within these book covers accessible for everyone.

First, the reflections on Christianity captured here will bring value to how you practice your faith in Jesus. Meaning this work is practical and applicable to your life, not just abstract theories reserved for philosophers and professors (Although I do enjoy geeking out on those things and it may slip out every so once in a while).

Second, the discussion of prayer is worth pondering. Prayer is one of the most basic and common practices of the Christian life. I ask some serious questions about prayer and try to give concrete examples for how to practice a richer prayer life.

Third, if you struggle with hypocritical Christians — people who say all the right stuff but act out anger, hate, prejudice, and other lifestyles counter to the way of Jesus — then the core concept of humility explored here is definitely for you. From Jesus' humble beginnings in the manger to the humble obedience to the mission of God even to dying on the cross, Jesus' most defining characteristic is humility. While I cannot fix your annoying family member or that Pharisee at your church, I do think the pages here will help with a self reflection. Are you humble?

Fourth, practical theology (PT). "In general terms, practical theology's four basic questions and task (as summarized by Princeton's Richard Osmer) are: what is going on? Why is this going on? What ought to be going on? How might we respond?"[1] Maybe you are interested in doing deep theological reflection on what scripture, tradition, and the Christian experience have to say about spiritual formation. I use three simple questions as part of my PT method in each chapter: now, know, and do. The now section asks the question: what is happening now? The know section of each chapter seeks to ask: what do we know about God? And finally, the practical section do asks: what should we try to do?

As you read, I hope you'll notice that we're revolving around one central idea: What does it mean to know God? I believe knowing God is much more intimate than the common imagination present in our churches. Prayer is more about listening than talking. Listening to God is only possible through a life marked by true humility. Living in true humility is grounded by gratitude. To be grounded in gratitude we need a new way to see our world that is unobstructed, this is possible through simplicity.

The chapters have been laid out in an intentional fashion, each one is enriched by the others. Along the way there will be moments of reflection and the encouragement to begin adding new practices to your life. If you are using this as a devotional book, I suggest you grab a journal or use the margins to capture insights and make notes for when you begin to craft your own rule of life or what I like to call a rhythm of life. The fifth chapter has some reflection questions to help guide you in crafting your own. As you are exposed to these new practices, I suggest you give yourself a trial period to test them out. In my opinion, these trial periods should last anywhere between one and three months.

---

1. Clark. *Adoptive Youth Ministry.* 97

May God hold you as you journey through the promptings and practices introduced here. May you offer your whole self up to trust in Jesus. And may you be filled with Holy Spirit wisdom to discern what is truly from God and to let go of what is not. Thanks for picking up this book!

Acknowledgements

TO MY PARENTS LARRY AND PAULA COBURN:

Dad, you are truly my Sensei, leadership coach, and role model. From being on the first eldership I served under and partnering in ministry the year you were the interim preaching minister to all the countless FaceTime calls and brainstorm sessions, thank you. And Mom, you not only raised me and Hans to remember who we are and who we belong to but taught us how to think, study, teach others, be kind, and humble. You instilled a deep curiosity of how people think and act, and a love for history. I am forever grateful to you both.

TO MY DAUGHTER ASHLYNN SELAH:

Thank you for helping me slow down and breathe.

TO MY WIFE JANEL:

You are my whole world. Thank you for using your skills in communication, grammar, writing, and speaking to make me a better writer and pastor. I am incredibly thankful for your constant patience and support as I muse and "play with" theological ideas. Thank you for not only sacrificing the time it took me to write this over the past four years but also the efforts you put in to edit and help me reshape the random ideas I had. I could not have done this without you. I love our life and I love doing life together with you. Thank you for rising to the challenge of love and marriage with me, I am truly a better person because of you. I love you to the moon and back Janel.

Introduction

Wanting: In Pursuit to Know God

On the sandy shores of the Sea of Galilee, Jesus was teaching. There were so many people and Jesus' words so captivating, they kept crowding in. Nearby some fishermen had pulled their boat on shore and were cleaning the nets. Jesus got into the boat belonging to Simon Peter and they floated out a little ways from shore and Jesus sat in the boat teaching the people. When Jesus finished preaching, he said "lets go out to the deep water and let down the nets." Peter was a bit tired. "Sir, we fished all night, and did not catch a thing. But because you have asked us to, we will put the nets out again."

So they let the nets down and caught an unbelievable amount of fish! Can you imagine the sound of these heavy nets full of fish slapping the water upon being pulled into the boat? Peter and Andrew begin yelling and hollering to their partners James and John. I am sure they wondered what the ruckus was all about. *There's no fish in this sea, we made sure of that last night.* I bet James and John wondered if they were sinking or something terrible had happened. So they rushed over. Rowing fast. Then came the marvelous sound of a thousand fins. They came along side and filled both boats to the point they had to start releasing fish in case they would sink or the nets would break.

When Peter finally had a chance to catch his breath and realize what just happened—the greatest catch of his life—he turned to Jesus, dropped to his knees, and cried "go away from me Lord, I am a sinful man!" Everyone was drop dead shocked and knew Jesus was the source of this miraculous and supernatural catch. Jesus said to Peter "Don't be afraid, from now on you will fish for people." When they pulled their boats on shore, they left everything and followed him.[1]

Who are you following? Every day someone is vying for you to follow them. Maybe it is your boss, a charismatic coworker, a team captain, choir director, friend on social media, celebrities, or politicians—these people want you to follow them when it comes to fashion, how you vote, the music you listen to, the books you read, the youtube channels you subscribe to, or the products you consume.

As of this morning while I write this, I have 256 followers on Instagram. Most of those followers are people I know personally, but some follow me simply because I tagged their friend in a post or checked in at a location they frequent. Some simply follow me because they want me to follow them back! When my wife and I got married a few years ago, my social media posts exploded with likes and comments. One photo had over 200 likes. But let's be honest, if I were simply on social media for likes and comments, I would have had to give up a long time ago. My 200 likes are nothing compared to the 18 million likes Kylie Jenner gets on a regular basis (and even her record was beaten by an Egg Photo one year).[2] People are often posting shots to get more and more likes. They attribute certain behavior or see it on others accounts that get them a lot of likes, so why not try it on mine they say. Whether it's a video of a crazy trick on a skateboard or bike that could get them killed or a picture that shows a bit more skin than the last one. The desire for more followers moves us to do things we never set out to do. And who we follow influences what we post and ultimately what we think is important and valuable in life. This is why celebrities get sponsored

1. Adapted from Luke 5:1–11 NIV

2. Jon Porter, "Egg Picture," The Verge, January 14, 2019, https://www.theverge.com/2019/1/14/18181806/instagram-most-liked-post-egg-kylie-jenner.

by companies to use their products, wear their clothes, and drive their cars. I have an awesome friend who reps for lululemon. He does Cross Fit, lives in Malibu, leads a great youth ministry, and serves as a campus minister. You could say I want to be like Dusty. So when I see him post about overcoming something challenging— like climbing a mountain or crushing a workout—I'm also seeing his lifestyle that includes lululemon. There have been times when I look into buying some lululemon products for myself; not because Dusty recommended the brand to me, but because I want to be like him and that's part of who he is. Who are you following? Who are you aspiring to be like? Who is influencing you?

Author and Christian thinker C. S. Lewis said this, "The whole purpose for which we exist is to be thus taken into the life of God. Wrong ideas about what that life is will make it harder."[3] You have probably heard the phrase, "when God made you he broke the mold." The American dream is that each of us can make a unique contribution to the world. No matter where you came from, everyone can become successful and "make it" with a little hard work and determination. The founding of our country was brought about by the American revolution. We read the stories of revolutionary heroes like George Washington, Ben Franklin, or Paul Revere and we want to be like them, we like to think we would have followed them on the revolutionary road to a "land of the free and home of the brave." Revolutionary leaders excite us and inspire us to be like them, whether it is Presidents like John F. Kennedy who inspired a country to put a man on the moon with "ask not what your country can do for you, ask what you can do for your country." Or civil rights leaders like Martin Luther King Jr. with his "I have a dream" speech. We are moved to follow revolutionaries. They invite us to see ourselves as unique and special. Modern day revolutionaries have capitalized on advances in technology. Apple founders Steve Jobs and Steve Wozniak revolutionized the computer industry with the dream that the individual could have the capabilities and resources only large organizations could afford. Apple and other companies promise us the ability to change the world on

---

3. Moon. *Apprenticeship with Jesus.* 29

our own. Youtube enables you create your own news, ideas, and other content allowing you to shape your audience without being a big network tv company. Almost every day there is some ad on my Facebook account recommending 10–12 step programs to help me get rich, self published, a new job, etc. The rise of the life coach, like Tony Robbins and others, shows how desperate people are to feel successful. Speaking of Facebook, Mark Zuckerberg practically became a millionaire over night! With the internet and technology, the promise every day is there for you and me to be another Mark Zuckerberg. . .But it doesn't happen that often does it? Speaker and leadership expert Simon Sinek says "People don't buy what you do, they buy why you do it." We all want to lead a revolutionary movement and change the world, but that may be more of a what. And the reason so many of us end up feeling burnt out, discouraged, and disappointed that our efforts to revolutionize our world fail is because we are focused on the what and not on why. Do we by chance have the wrong idea about the life God created us for? It is hard to enter into this creative life God has called us to when we have the wrong ideas about what that creative life looks like.

Derek Sivers shares some amazing leadership advice over a video of a dancing shirtless dude, he says:

> Leadership is over glorified. It was the first follower who transformed a lone nut into a leader. We are told we all need to be leaders but that would be really ineffective. The best way to make a movement, if you really care, is to courageously follow and show others how to follow. When you find a lone nut doing something great, be the first to person to standup and join in.[4]

One of the most influential Christian revolutionaries was Paul, he was a sort of first follower of Jesus. He brought the Christian movement to new places all over the world. This is how he describes his leader:

> 15 The Son is the image of the invisible God, the firstborn over all creation. 16 For in him all things were created:

4. Derek Sivers, "First Follower," Derek Sivers, February 11, 2010, https://sivers.org/ff.

things in heaven and on earth, visible and invisible, whether thrones or powers or rulers or authorities; all things have been created through him and for him. 17 He is before all things, and in him all things hold together. 18 And he is the head of the body, the church; he is the beginning and the firstborn from among the dead, so that in everything he might have the supremacy. 19 For God was pleased to have all his fullness dwell in him, 20 and through him to reconcile to himself all things, whether things on earth or things in heaven, by making peace through his blood, shed on the cross. . . .24 Now I rejoice in what I am suffering for you, and I fill up in my flesh what is still lacking in regard to Christ's afflictions, for the sake of his body, which is the church. 25 I have become its servant by the commission God gave me to present to you the word of God in its fullness— 26 the mystery that has been kept hidden for ages and gen- erations, but is now disclosed to the Lord's people. 27 To them God has chosen to make known among the Gen- tiles the glorious riches of this mystery, which is Christ in you, the hope of glory.28 He is the one we proclaim, admonishing and teaching everyone with all wisdom, so that we may present everyone fully mature in Christ. 29 To this end I strenuously contend with all the energy Christ so powerfully works in me.[5]

Paul knows his goal—the what—is to revolutionize and create transformed people. But he does not get lost in goal setting, instead he chose to focus on his why: *Christ in you the hope of glory.* This crucial statement means two things. First, *Christ in you* means God is not somewhere far far away but close and personal. Paul believes God in the Spirit of Christ comes and sets up shop in your heart. Elsewhere Paul is found to say "it is no longer I who live but Christ who lives in me."[6] Second, *the hope of glory* speaks to the expect- ant reality we live with about being with God. Right now we have questions and experience distance and disconnect but one day we will know God fully and feel fully known by God. Glory is the awe

5. Colossians 1:15–29 NIV
6. Galatians 2:20 NIV

and wonder of God's presence. We often describe moments of the Glory of God being expressed in the miracles of the Bible, a beautiful sunset, or a particularly meaningful worship experience. The glory Paul speaks of here is the true glory which awaits us in the end when we no longer "look through a glass darkly" but instead "see face to face."[7] Paul lives with the trust of knowing Christ lives inside him even though at times he gets in the way, so he holds onto the expectant hope of one day his heart will be in complete unity with the Spirit of Christ. For now he models for us what it means to follow Jesus and live the life God has called each of us to live. The good news of Jesus is not about leading it is about being led. To change the world, to create a revolution you need to be a good follower who leaves your day job, fishing with nets, to follow the true revolutionary and change people's lives.

THE REVOLUTION

You are created to create a revolution. But so much of the messaging in our world today is that we have to create our own image. An image of success and power. Henri Nouwen, a catholic missionary, scholar, former Harvard professor, and renowned author knew the temptation all too well to settle for creating our own image which means we miss out on changing the world. He writes this in a book about the Temptations of Jesus:

> What makes the temptation of power so seemingly irresistible? Maybe it is that power offers an easy substitute for the hard task of love. It seems easier to be God than to love God, easier to control people than to love people, easier to own life than to love life. Jesus asks, "Do you love me?" We ask, "Can we sit at your right hand and your left hand in your Kingdom?" (Matthew 20:21). Ever since the snake said, "The day you eat of this tree your eyes will be open and you will be like gods, knowing good from evil" (Genesis 3:5), we have been tempted to replace love with power. The long painful history of the church is the history of people ever and again tempted to

7. 1 Corinthians 13:12 KJV

choose power over love, control over the cross, being a leader over being led.[8]

Nouwen's words are heavy. To truly transform the world of Genesis 3, one where God's creation is broken and in need of a revolution, we need to move from being leaders to being led. God has gifted you with tremendous talents and a life to create something, but the messages bombarding us each day are temptations of power, to use our gifts and talents to create our own image rather than follow Jesus, the revolutionary who leads us all back into being the true image bearers of God, the way we were created. People need to see followers of Jesus being creative and being with God. You cannot help others follow Jesus if you are never with Jesus. You will just end up having them follow you. You were created to create a revolution, but we often fail to change the world because the movement becomes about us and our image, power, and control rather than about our why: *Christ in you, the hope of glory.* Our why leads to prison walls being broken down, poverty dispelled, wounds attended to, and smiles on strained and stressed out faces because Christ is in us. We love rather than control because we are being led rather than leading, we are following Jesus, the image of God. This is a movement worth leaving everything for.

WHAT DO YOU WANT?

San Diego is an amazing city. Flying in over downtown is quite the experience landing beside the beautiful harbor. I remember grabbing my bag as I stood up in the aisle of the plane not sure what awaited in this new place. I was twenty two years old on my first full time job interview. About a month before I had received an email back from a church. They were willing to look past the fact I was about to graduate with a Bachelors degree in accounting but was pursuing a position in Youth Ministry. The idea of moving to San Diego could not have been better. My fiancé was moving home to Orange County after graduation and our wedding was still months away. I thanked the flight crew in between thoughts about what this

8. Nouwen, *In the Name of Jesus.* 59–60

job might mean for my future. Down the escalator stood a man holding a paper sign with my name on it. His name was Dan. We got in the car that temperate January day in San Diego headed for a youth event at the ice rink. On the drive we chatted, and thinking back now the conversation was very typical for the two of us. We exchanged overseas stories, especially about Taiwan, with his role as an engineer and my dad's work with Nike which relocated us to Taiwan in the mid 90's. Pulling up to the mall I would later live next door to, Dan asked me if there was anything I wanted to ask him as one of the elders since the rest of my weekend would be with the search committee. You can read books, get advice from mentors, and pray hard for God to speak but few things can help you overcome the desire within you to get what you want. Dan asked a very good question and had I been prepared for it our relationship might have been radically different. Not even a year later I would reflect, if I had been prepared for his question, would I have continued to pursue the job? Had I known that day what I know now, would I have still accepted? Now don't get me wrong San Diego is one of my favorite places on the planet! I lived in two apartments, both of which I was able to run to the ocean from. In response to Dan's question I shrugged and said "is there anything you want to know about me?"

Life is a series of choices. Every day we make thousands of them. What should I eat? How should I respond to what you just asked me? What takes priority in my life? The question "what do you want" can be perplexing. Go ahead, make a list of all the things you want, you will probably start off strong but can you really name all of the things you want? It is more intuitive, a development over time. We moved back home to Portland, Oregon after 18 months in Manila, Philippines in 1998 when I was seven. Sometime in that first year I began to request my hamburgers without ketchup. If you asked me what I wanted to eat I would tell you clearly "I want a cheeseburger without ketchup." If you were lucky I said please and thank you, but if you failed to remember the no ketchup rule I was not going to eat it. For the life of me I do not remember why this started, years later as I began to realize how absurd it was I began to craft a story of why. There is probably some truth to the story, but I have no doubt I began to embellish the story to justify my odd desire. I still find myself using this story to explain away my odd dislike for ketchup. In the Philippines the ketchup is made from a banana base, which causes it to have a sweet flavor. Many people who like normal ketchup find the sweet ketchup difficult to get used to. Apparently I used to consume quite a bit of ketchup without complaint during our expatriate years in Taiwan and the Philippines, it was only after we moved back to Oregon that I began to develop an aversion to ketchup. My aversion to ketchup is a trivial example, but bears a great symbolism to the greater issue of behaviors we see in people every day. I discovered that what I wanted was flavored different so I actively chose to avoid anything that did not satisfy my desire. Children are the best models of this. I have several nephews and nieces five and under, who are currently coming into the communication development stage. Language becomes a tool they master as they develop clearer lines of communicating what they want and need. The adults in the room often burst out laughing when one of the little ones tries hard to tell a parent or other adult what they want. Sometimes a parent will restate what the perceived desire is so the child learns to pronounce it correctly, or sometimes there is a lesson of self discipline and the child is expected to finish dinner before the ice cream sandwich can be consumed. We smile and laugh at their adorable attempts at language, and sometimes temper tantrums, while they try to convey what they want. (Usually having something to do with food or a toy Uncle Lars has snatched up and is withholding.)

Do you have a ketchup story? Or maybe you have a toddler around who is learning to express their desires in funny ways. Adult life is really no different. We may have the whole of the english language—and for some of you several languages—at our disposal but we still struggle to express what we truly want. Communication is not easy. John Maxwell, a prolific author on leadership, noticed a phenomenon amongst people. He captures his thoughts in a book called *Everyone Communicates, Few Connect*. This is my nephew's struggle when he shouts "I wan dat" and points adamantly at the food on the adults plate from his vantage in the high chair. Ignoring his own portion of food, he melts down when his parents ask a clarifying question: "what is it you want? You already have food." He is communicating but he is not connecting. Maybe you have not begun screaming or melting down into a temper tantrum at the office, but how many times have you tried to tell your boss "I want that raise". How about at home? With your spouse or significant other. You have been together for months or years, and you wonder why he hasn't gotten you those flowers. Why she ignores your affectionate advances, or does not return the back scratches. Haven't I communicated what I want? "I want that" you say to your buddies at the basketball court. "I don't understand how he's so dense" you tell the marriage counselor. Truth be told, you have communicated but have you really connected?

At ten years old if you had asked me what I wanted at a burger joint or fast food restaurant, I would have told you adamantly I wanted my cheeseburger without ketchup. If the restaurant messed up my order, game over. But you know what, it had nothing really to do with ingredients. I was a super happy camper if you got me a hamburger smothered in barbecue sauce. If you take a bottle of ketchup and barbecue sauce (Sweet Baby Rays is a personal favorite) the ingredients read exactly the same. Both are tomato based, with high fructose corn syrup nearly the exact same quantities. The difference? Flavoring additives. That's it! The real purpose behind my distaste for ketchup was the desire to be seen and known. I thought communicating with others was the same as connecting with them. Even at a young age I desired to be recognized by the people in my life. How do you know if people acknowledge you, you ask them to do something specific for you. I was evaluating relationships based on communication with people, by if they remembered I did not like ketchup. Today I still do not like ketchup on my fries—my poor wife realized the other day we don't even have a bottle in our fridge for the times she wants to cook some good meatloaf. Over the years my anti ketchup phase has led me to realize I could communicate my distaste for ketchup to everyone in the world but it did little to connect me with them. Oh here and there a person would find my habit strange or interesting enough to ask probing questions. But today I approach connection differently. In a restaurant I often ask the server or person I am out to lunch or dinner with what they recommend and 90% of the time I order that exactly. If I am out with a large group, I pour more energy into conversation about food rather than pouring over the menu trying to discover what I want. My wife and I share meals at almost every opportunity, and it has become a fun way to connect deeper. She knows that if we are having french fries to keep the ketchup on her side of the plate, but the connection is much deeper than her knowing just to avoid ketchup for me. Janel and I can order for the other without hesitation because we have moved on from just communicating our dislikes or likes to connecting with each others desires.

My first ministry position came with a huge learning curve. Over time, I've come to realize that my frustrations were not with actual people in that setting; it was with God. I felt lost, I had told people God gave me a calling to ministry. I had convinced myself that God wanted me to be the youth minister in San Diego, but now this was not what I wanted. What changed? Why do I feel disconnected from God? I pray, read my Bible, go to church —I am communicating with God— but I do not seem to be connecting.

TO KNOW GOD

Connection with God, really knowing God, is more than just simply communicating, or what we call prayer. It is a journey, and journeys usually take longer than we would like and often plan for. Knowing God is vast and complex, but also beautiful and simple. My hope is that as you dig into the reflections and suggestions found here you will "seek first the kingdom of God" and let everything else be handled by your loving God, our Heavenly and good Parent. I did not write this book to be a how to guide for churches or pastors to become better at prayer. Rather, I am regurgitating the journey I have been on and the reflections I have received from those ahead of me on this journey who I want to emulate. I pass them on to you with the same adage the Apostle Paul said, "imitate me, as I imitate Christ."[9] The journey I have taken is to realize talking my way through life means all I ever hear is my own voice. The best

9. 1 Corinthians 11:1 NIV

marriage advice I have ever heard is: listen to your wife because listening paves the way for true intimacy. I am convinced that in order to truly know God we must be humble and listen more than we speak. To do that we need to be thankful which grounds this life with God. Too often we fail to see due to the noise and busyness of our lives which is why we need to embrace practices that help simplify our lives. All of these will change the way we relate to God, especially our prayer life.

BLESSING

May the words here bring you closer to know the love of God the Father.

As you seek truth, may you be guarded from unhealthy and unholy thinking.

May absolute joy fill your life because of the hope found in Jesus your friend and savior.

As you pursue justice, may you not waver, clearly rooted in the power of the resurrection.

May light be your guide as the Holy Spirit fills you and you bear much fruit.

As you live, may you not be discouraged, but strengthened by Holy Spirit power.

May the Grace of the Lord Jesus, The Love of God the Father, And the Friendship of our Guide the Holy Spirit be with you always! Amen

Chapter 1

Faith: Shaping How We Relate to God

NOW: WHAT IS HAPPENING NOW? | SPIRITUAL FORMATION

Spiritual formation is a catchy phrase, but what does it mean? The first church I worked full time for in San Diego had an entire staff member assigned to spiritual formation. It might be a sort of "I know it when I see it" phrase. Take the words for a moment; spiritual might mean some sort of belief system (aka religion or faith) and formation conjures up images of a lump of clay that the artist forms or molds into a shape. With these definitions, we could define spiritual formation as the shaping of faith or the molding of a belief system. What is the shape of your faith? How do you describe your spiritual state of being? Another way to look at it would be to cast it in developmental terms. How developed is your belief system? In most countries we have a systematic approach to educating children as they develop and grow into mature adults. My grandmother described her education as focusing on the three "r's" of reading, writing, and arithmetic (I know, I know they do not actually start with the letter r). Her lament was that we have complicated our education system so much these days. Why has that happened? Well it actually could be coming from a good place. The public school in San Diego my wife taught first grade at was called a STEAM school. This meant their focus was on science, technology, engineering, art, and math. She taught the first graders how to read, write, and do arithmetic in the context of units of learning surrounding science, technology, engineering, art, and math. She taught historical figures from the standpoint of how they impacted a particular aspect of STEAM subjects. The maturing and learning, or formation, might seem complex but it is actually incredibly intentional. I believe the same can be said of spiritual formation. We should not shy away from more complex ways of understanding how our faith is formed, especially the practices affirmed throughout the history of the Christian tradition. Yet much of what is happening today is rejecting the rich array of spiritually forming and maturing activities in favor a more juvenile approach.

I have found this as a helpful definition for spiritual formation: any and all ways your attentiveness to God is shaped. This may seem confusing. Many of us use relationship language to talk about God —how is your relationship with God, do you have a relationship with Jesus, or I want you to get to know God— but what does that mean? I have many different kinds of relationships. I have a relationship with my wife that is special, unique, and intimate. This relationship involves tremendous amounts of communication, complex history, dependence on each other, physical interaction (sexual and non-sexual), shared space, emotions (the ups and downs), desires (what do I want from her and what does she want from me), and commitments (marriage, honesty, accountability, attention, etc). Other human relationships have some various overlaps and even some unique things, such as my relationship with my boss involves financial things and work ethic. Let us take it a step further, I love my dog and have a relationship with her. Few would say, however, that this relationship is the same kind of relationship as the one I have with other people, or even remotely the same intimacy level as with my wife. Even more so, the relationship I have with the fish in the bowl that sits in our kitchen is further removed.

I talk to the fish just like I talk to the dog, and neither of them talk back. The dog communicates to some degree by scratching at the door or occasionally barking for attention. The reality is this: talking about God as someone we are meant to have a relationship with is unhelpful at best. At worst, it is misleading. Yes we want to simplify things. Complexity does not make something automatically better. But have we reduced the shaping of our faith to a well intentioned bumper sticker or slogan that lacks any real substance? I have taught classes and led youth camps where the message was: God created you to be in relationship with Him and this is how to do that. Funny enough we often use three "r's": repentance (or change), reading (the Bible), and relationship (talking to God in prayer). Like my grandmother's summation of the centrality of basic education being reading, writing, and arithmetic I agree that the three "r's" of faith are central, I just do not see them as being formative in the current approaches most widely propagated.

I have a curiosity about how people think about faith. I am intrigued that so many want to distance themselves from being labeled religious but still hold onto many religious habits and world views. Many people, if asked about their relationship with God, might use language given to them by their spiritual mentors or communities. We are being formed every day by the messages that surround us: television shows, movies, songs, phrases from influencers in our life (pastors, parents, mentors, teachers, peers, and celebrities), and the books we read. To eliminate relationship from our language when we talk about faith and God is unrealistic, it is the water we swim in or the air we breathe. This is how people naturally talk about faith, but in trying to simplify everything we allowed ourselves to come to a juvenile understanding of what that relationship is. All the complex liturgies—liturgy is a fancy way of saying order of worship service—in the more traditional churches are composed of three basic elements. 1) Repentance: admitting that we are not where we ought to be and need to change. 2) Reading: hearing the Bible read aloud or quoting it to each other. 3) Relationship: prayers of confession, petition, praise, and *gratitude*. Less complex Christian gatherings are also full of these three things. When we encourage people to set aside time to be with God we usually ask about the things that they need to change in their life (repentance), the Bible reading they are or are not doing daily (reading), and how often they pray—or "talk to God" (relationship). I have fallen into this trap so often as a way to feel good that I helped someone by prescribing "just talk to God about it more."

KNOW: WHAT DO WE KNOW ABOUT GOD? | ETERNAL LIFE

What is wrong with this prescription of repentance, reading, and relationship? Let us revisit the various relationships we discussed earlier. The Bible discusses marriage as being something that points to the divine mystery of God's trinitarian relationship out of which God created humanity. Jesus in John 14 uses groom proposal language —"in my fathers house are many rooms. . .I am going there to prepare a place for you. . ."— when he tells his followers of his coming departure by death on the cross. Jesus speaks like a husband, which I believe is why this language is then continued in the book of Revelation by the Apostle John. John identifies himself as "the Disciple whom Jesus loved" and in his shorter letters notes that we are the "beloved children of God." The Apostle Paul gives some helpful marriage relational advice to husbands and wives regarding love and respecting each other just to conclude the section in Ephesians with a statement "but I am speaking of Christ and the church." The church is noted as the bride of Christ, very intimate language here. So when we preach or teach that the whole reason for our existence is to be in relationship with God we do so with this marriage analogy handed to us. Scripture paints this picture of incredible intimacy in regards to a relationship with God, yet we act so nonchalant around God.

Friends, acquaintances, coworkers, and supervisors all require less face time, communication, and all around work than our spouses. For those of you who are not married, you have probably observed couples with marital strife, the simplest comment or action can be the straw that breaks the back. Living together can be the best and worst thing for the relationship. This, I believe, is why so many couples are living together before marriage and why co-habitation is so common, because younger people have witnessed too many miserable and unhappy marriages, and want to have a trial period. I would like to say there is an easy solution, but every day I have a choice set before me whether to choose to love my wife or find some reason why I am irritated. Some days the choice is easier and some days the choice is more difficult, but it is always there. Marriage is a lot of work. I spend the most face to face human interaction with my wife and she is also the one I text the most, the one I most frequently call, and the one I fight with the most. Marriage is not a climb up a mountain with some valleys on the way but rather more like a heart rate monitor beeping up and down. Some of the highs are really high, and the lows are often really low, but the most defining characteristic is the short span of time between the two. A relationship without frequent volatile highs and lows, perhaps back to back in the same day, may not be breathing. It is the rhythm of daily life and the grind of doing laundry, cooking meals, staying out of debt, the tug and pull of careers, and the complexity of emotions at any given moment that make for deep intimacy and a beautiful sexual relationship. I use the term sexual knowing which in common vernacular refers to intercourse but the term can also apply to how we relate with others through interpersonal communication. Much of the Bible was written originally in Hebrew, and the word that our English translations often use for sex could be literally translated "know." For instance, in some older English translations of the Bible it says "Adam knew his wife and she became pregnant. . ."[1] If you have had the sex talk, then you know where babies come from and most of you will answer that simply knowing someone, in our way of using language today, does not mean you had sex with them. We have reduced deep intimacy and knowing of another to simply knowing information about them. I might see a picture on your Instagram account, watch a few snapchat stories, read your political Facebook rant, or drink an over priced coffee across from you and say I "know" you, but do I know you? Have I truly intermingled my soul with yours?

1. Genesis 4:1 KJV

They say it's not what you know, it's who you know. In my studies at graduate school and work in ministry I have come to experience just how true this really is! So much of what might be explained as being in the right place at the right time is setup by the hard daily work of getting to know others. Leadership expert John Maxwell coaches people to ask great questions, and one that he passed on is to always ask, "Who do you know that I should know?"[2] This is a fascinating faith shaping question. Jesus says that when the Spirit of God comes, his followers will receive power and be witnesses in Jerusalem, Judea, Samaria, and the ends of the earth.[3] Jesus says you will be given the ability to live in such a way that people want to ask: who do you know that I should know? Our response to this is to introduce them—to witness—to Jesus the one we know intimately. This witnessing starts right here and now and extends out to everywhere and every moment. When the relationship is superficial, like the ones we have with other humans, the transformative power will not be seen and no one will ask the question, "Who do you know that I should know?" This requires hard work.

Research has pointed out that teenagers are exhibiting a faith that is described as moralistic therapeutic deism (MTD)[4]. Kenda Creasy Dean says "we" as adults "are to blame" because young people are following and adopting the faith they see and experience in churches.[5] One of my former youth group students remarked during our month on prayer, "So prayer is like a text message and God never replies." At the time I felt like this student was attacking me but I learned quickly that as a wrestler and A+ student, challenge was his way of processing and learning. Reflecting on

2. John C. Maxwell, "Minute With Maxwell," https://www.youtube.com/watch?v=yZ-leOj9aoE.

3. Acts 1:8 NIV

4. Definition of MTD: "It is moralistic, meaning that religious young people equate faith with being a good, moral person (genrally, being nice). It is therapeutic, so faith becomes a means of feeling better about themselves. And it is deistic, meaning God exists, but this God is not involved in human affairs with any regularity." Powell. *Growing Young.* 130

5. Ibid., *Growing Young.* 133

the experience later, I realized the real reason I felt attacked was because I did not agree that was how prayer really works but he had just named my own prayer life. How many times have you gotten a message back from God? Some of you will be able to name times when God answered prayers or you heard a clear message from God; good! This means you have the capacity and language to name how God speaks to you. This is important and healthy, a very real part of molding belief. The thing is, we often only know what God is saying in hind sight or the rear view mirror.

When we ask the dog if they need to go to the bathroom, knowing full well they cannot actually speak back to us, we feel affirmed when we open the door and they promptly go out to do their business. Dogs have emotions and use nudges, sounds, and general intuition to communicate with us when they need to go out and when they need to eat. We often treat our relationship with God this way almost as if God is some sort of mute, distant, aloof entity that we think is predictable. Dogs are great, they make us happy and bring joy into our lives, but unlike people we do not have to work very hard. A dog will forget what just happened in a very short period of time. They never talk back or correct you. A dog will do its own thing, so what about the hard work of relationship building? If you feed the dog it will love you. I sense that we bring this into our relationship with God all the time. Within Christianity it is a bit more difficult to see the trappings of this behavior still evident, but it is there in full force. When I lived in Vietnam, many families were still Buddhist even under Communist enforced atheism. Going to a tailor, coffee shop, local business, or buddhist family home you would see a small altar or shrine that included an image of a god or goddess and fresh fruit with incense burning. The fruit is a sacrifice, an offering, to gain the approval or favor of the gods. This has been carried out for centuries by religious groups of different faith communities. We see God as something to be controlled, manipulated into giving us what we want or feel we deserve. God is so much more than something to be used to our own advantage. It is easy to see this in the superstitious practices of ancient religions or the more mystical traditions of our times, but there is a thin line of difference between them and the modern church theology of praise and worship. We might not set out to control God, but our habits and song lyrics betray the subconscious behavior we are operating from. When crisis hits we pray and ask God to heal, because we want God to fix this situation. We sing songs praising God that culminate with clapping and cheering, a worship leader who softly prays about how we feel God's presence, and that we want more relationship with God. We think that a good set of music, a smoke machine, some lights, and catchy words will bring God more into our lives. We speak to God as if his presence is something new, something that needs to be brought places. We talk about God's mission and heart for the lost as something we make happen. God becomes a passive actor in our lives, at best God is like an aloof dog in our worship services nudging us through intuitive communication but at worst God is like the token fish in a bowl.

My wife and I got married at a beautiful golf course in San Juan Capistrano, California and, as you would expect, Orange County weddings usually cost thousands of dollars. So you can imagine we shopped around. One option was to get married on a yacht, these triple decker boats make for a beautiful venue. While we considered it for quite some time, the deciding factor was, like all good decisions, about food! We ended up loving our venue because they allowed us to bring in an In N Out truck! We had several mementos at our wedding remembering grandparents who have passed and a beta fish. Someone has to feed the fish and regularly change the fishes water. We have since bought several environmental objects to improve the fish's life experience. At the time of writing this, nearly three years since our wedding, the fish is still with us. The fish has undergone moves, dozens of car rides, and even a near death leap out of the bowl into a coffee cup. Our family feels a sense of attachment to this fish, we talk to the fish, observe the fish, ask about how the fish is doing, and even change our schedules to hand the fish off. We have a relationship with this fish. It represents our wedding, a symbol connecting us with other people. But do I know the fish? Of course I know about it, I know what it is called, I know where the fish is, but is this really relationship? Is God like a fish on your kitchen counter? God may have a prominent place in our homes, we may talk a lot about God too. Like the fish which has a special place in my family and connects us together, God is often a topic of discussion and part of the heritage of our family. We attend to our faith in God by displaying it prominently in our lives: public prayers before meals, Bibles on our coffee tables, and going to Bible studies. We clean the fish bowl and maintain our faith in God by reading Christian books, listening to good Bible teaching and preaching, and confessing our struggles. We spend a lot of time planning out our spirituality: which church we will attend, how often we will go, what special events or seminars we will go to, Bible reading plans, and service efforts to be part of. Like spending money on a fish we do not really know, we exert tremendous financial, physical, and relational efforts on a God who is really more of a token than someone we know intimately. Is this too harsh an assessment?

C.S. Lewis is right that having the wrong idea about what a life with God means will make it near impossible to actually experience that life. We spend all our energy and time cleaning the bowl of our faith and no time listening to God, why? Frankly it is because we know the fish cannot talk back. In the evening Janel often asks me who I talked to during the day. I usually share about the FaceTime calls with my parents, the meetings with church members—you know other humans. We have a pretend imagination for what our little dog's personality is like. We make up words and pretend to talk for her, so when my wife gets home she asks about the dog as well. Throughout the day I have interacted with the dog and interpret that through words. So it would not be cause for distress if she walked in as I was sitting in front of the dog staring at her in silence, for I could respond in all seriousness to her questions about what I was doing with: "I am listening to her." I might even be able to make some meaning based on the dog's behavior and mood so that when my wife asks "and what is she saying to you" to respond "she's lonely." However, if my wife came home and found me staring at the fish bowl and asked "what are you doing" to which I respond similar to the dog situation she would not be wrong to call a shrink. Depending on the severity of my commitment and devotion to the fact the fish will actually communicate back, you would probably agree I needed help (or you might think I was being aided by some sort of drug already and need to detox). Yet, this is how many of us approach spirituality and we do not call each other out on the absurdity because it has become normalized. Call it divine luck, destiny, fate, karma, mysticalness, a higher power, God, or some other belief system—we all approach life a bit superstitious. In the moment of a religious experience we might affirm that God is active and real. We sing about knowing God intimately and read about God being in us, but that does not translate into our day to day reality. Not all readers will feel this way, the fastest growing expression of Christianity today is one that gives people a language to express supernatural ways God acts in their lives right now.

The Enlightenment, a philosophical shift in the 1600's to 1800's, brought helpful and unhelpful things. We came to understand gravity and scientific inquiry flourished, leading us to technological advances capable of designing the rocket which took a man off the planet to the moon! Still, while science was actually advanced by people of faith, the fruit was a continued dissatisfaction with the mystery of God and a relationship with God. This highly logical and reason based way of thinking meant we moved away from talking about having visions about encountering God or Jesus to forms of check lists that one can teach and follow to know for certain you know God. The complex heartbeat ups and downs of an intimate relationship were replaced with a method to know about, care, and display faith in God in our lives. For those who did not grow up in the Churches of Christ, one of the great frontier revival preachers of the 1800's in North America noted a pattern in the Bible that became and still is often how people are taught to convert to Christianity. The five steps, or originally the five finger exercise, was: 1) hear, 2) believe, 3) repent, 4) confess, 5) be baptized. First, one must hear that they need a savior and who Jesus is. Then they must believe it; not just in God but in Jesus as the son of God.[6] This hearing and believing should lead to a realization of their sin, or separation from God, and need to change their life.[7] Confession is not like in the movies about Roman Catholics seeing

---

6. Romans 10; John 3

7. Acts 2

the priest and telling all of the horrible things they have done, but rather confessing their belief that Jesus is the Christ, the Son of God in front of others.[8] We declare the "Good Confession" to others usually right before or at the time of our baptism (the final of the five steps). Baptism is this ancient tradition of being fully immersed in water to represent our dying to our old life, being buried like Jesus was, and rising to the new life promised for those in Christ.[9] The Bible demonstrates this pattern over and over; it is very reasonable, it is beautiful, and it places God at the center of our life. The confidence in this five step method was based on the ability to cite verses from the Bible to support the pattern. But does this really give us confidence in knowing God?

Remember John? The Apostle who describes himself as the one whom Jesus loved? The guy who uses the bride language? The one who seems to want us to know the most important way of viewing ourselves is as God's beloved. John captures the longest teaching of Jesus, and the most in depth. We often think about the Sermon on the Mount being Jesus' pinnacle speech, but John actually presents a longer teaching section around a table and in a garden just before Jesus goes to the cross. John 17, the end of this lengthy teaching section, is the only extended prayer of Jesus' we have recorded. The Lord's prayer is teaching on how to pray and all the others are short phrases or descriptions of where Jesus prayed. From a literary perspective, the prayer in John is more like a dissertation and last teaching. John recalls Jesus' prayer as a teaching moment for us regarding the tangibility of Jesus' relationship with God. The opening line has Jesus doing something very familiar to our religious experience: addressing God as Father. Jesus then talks to God about what faith is. "Now this is eternal life: that they know you, the only true God, and Jesus Christ, whom you have sent."[10] There is that sticky word and concept again. Jesus says it with such conviction he cannot simply mean know about.

8. Matthew 16

9. Romans 6

10. John 17:3 NIV

This is the crisis in spiritual formation and religion in general. We have the wrong idea about what knowing God means. We may use language that describes God as our intimate friend who loves us in the mystery of the deepest ways through and through. But when it comes to practice we resign to placing God on the kitchen counter. We leave spiritual retreats or mountain top experiences where others modeled or told us about times they experienced God's nudging and intuitively knew it was God working in their life. They say things like "God told me to move here, enroll in seminary, quit my job, marry this person. . .etc" and with the benefit of it being something in the past we can intellectually make the leap to affirm that their experience was one in which God communicated clearly. We like things clean cut and not messy. Like when the dog scratches on the door, nudging us to let her out to go do her business. We feel good when she finds the right patch of grass and our interpretation of the scratch is confirmed. In my marriage I wish the non verbal cues were this easy to interpret. The reality is that the intimacy we desire requires a daily heart beat of ups and downs, often the dramatic ones actually signify the relationship is alive and beating. A flat line might sound nice for a relationship, always knowing what to expect, no surprises, but when it comes to the human body a flat line means you're dead. A relationship with no volatility is often a dead relationship. Outside forces, like CPR, defibrillators, pace makers, and heart medication can provide rhythm and life when the body is no longer functioning right, but all of them are temporary at best. An intimate relationship can also have outside forces artificially boost life and add rhythm, but they are no substitute for the natural heart beat of a healthy relationship between people who truly know one another and become one. This is the mystery of marriage and intimacy that points us to God. Paul describes it as the great hope and mystery made known now: Christ in you, which is the hope of God's ultimate reality (or glory in our translations). God's most prized creation is the relationship with humanity. But we often settle for knowing about God and assuming that listening for God to speak is foolish.

Spiritual formation then must be about much more than knowing about God or forming habits that maintain the fishbowl we have placed God in. Spiritual formation must be more than interpreting the scratches at the doors of our lives and reframing things. So many Christians I know quote Romans 8 to me whenever any little discomfort comes or a bad decision goes array and say: "God has a reason I know it, we just cannot see what it is yet." Oh that the emphasis would not be on that word "yet." If we believe God is in us, intimately in relationship with us then the communication should be clear right? God is in us, Spirit speaking to our spirit. Jesus says we are his friends, "I no longer call you servants, for servants do not know the masters will. But now I have called you friends, for everything my Father has revealed to me I have made known to you."[11]

My wife and I do not mean to hurt each others feelings, and usually the hurt feelings is more about a bunch of factors and there is often no clear resolution to the matter. The ones that go deep do not really resolve themselves in a neat logical way. But the moment I shutdown and refuse to talk the matter over with my wife the relationship is strained, the beautiful part of conflict is when we listen to each other, not when we prove our point or agree. Agreement is different than understanding. Knowing my wife more and more, means that I must listen; listen to understand not necessarily agree. Why do we believe we have to always agree with God? Why do we believe God has a plan but do not spend any time listening for what the plan is? Spiritual formation today does a great job of keeping God in a prominent place in our lives but ends up shaping our faith into a fish bowl for God to swim around in on display.

Spiritual formation in the robust situations of mission focused people and organizations gets closer to the mark. Spending enough time with the practices of prayer you condition yourself to turn to prayer at any and all times. This is good and might even be what the Apostle Paul implores when he tells the church at Thessaloniki to "pray continually" or as the older translations often put it "pray without ceasing." But does talking to the air, repeating phrases, closing your eyes, or even meditating actually imply you know God? Ruth Haley Barton calls this sort of intense prayer life one

11. John 15:15 NIV

of "striving" and not resting with God. We are again faced with the reality that reading the Bible, prayer, going to church, and mission for God can actually result in a life that looks to be one with God but is so busy God is not truly known. Author and Catholic father Richard Rohr writes regarding life being divided into two halves. The first half needs rules, rituals, and strict habits to adequately form the container for our identities. In *Falling Upward* he writes that many, if not most, never reach the second half of life, because it is not something one achieves or can program the transition, rather it is a fall. A life with God, one where we no longer strive within the first half of life's rules and strict practices, is something we must fall into. This may feel like I am giving up after all that was presented here. While there is not a set of exact patterns to follow in order to break through to truly knowing God in the intimacy we desire, I believe Jesus holds the key. In his life there seems to be three key virtues: *humility, gratitude,* and *simplicity.* These three virtues empower prayer as a way to know God. Let us return to Jesus as our example for life with God.

DO: WHAT SHOULD WE TRY TO DO? | LISTEN

The Apostles knew that Jesus was not just a good prophet who called us to "repent" and they knew he was not some other non-earthly being (like Superman or an alien) but treated him as an example.[12] In the Gospels Jesus continually invites people from all walks of life to follow him. John records Jesus' powerful statement "whoever believes in me will do the works I have been doing, and they will do even greater things than these, because I am going to the Father."[13] This theme of Jesus being an example is especially potent in the Apostle Paul's writing. The letter to the church at Rome is often said to be Paul's Gospel or the most complete Pauline theology. In chapter four Paul sets Jesus up as the second Adam, the type set for the new humanity as the first Adam is the type set for the old humanity under sin, law, and death. Jesus, as the second Adam, is the ideal

12. Mark 1:14 NIV
13. John 14: 12 NIV

human and example for who Paul believes all Christians should be. Paul uses this same theme in his first letter to the Corinthians when he writes "Imitate me as I imitate Christ."[14] While these passages reveal Paul's commitment, like the other Apostles and authors of the New Testament, to Jesus being an example, no passage is more explicit about what kind of example Jesus has set for us than Philippians chapter two.

> Therefore if you have any encouragement from being united with Christ, if any comfort from his love, if any common sharing in the Spirit, if any tenderness and compassion, then make my joy complete by being like-minded, having the same love, being one in spirit and of one mind. Do nothing out of selfish ambition or vain conceit. Rather, in *humility* value others above your-selves, not looking to your own interests but each of you to the interests of the others. In your relationships with one another, have the same mindset as Christ Jesus: Who, being in very nature God, did not consider equality with God something to be used to his own advantage; rather, he made himself nothing by taking the very nature of a servant, being made in human likeness. And being found in appearance as a man, he humbled himself by becom-ing obedient to death—even death on a cross! Therefore God exalted him to the highest place and gave him the name that is above every name, that at the name of Jesus every knee should bow, in heaven and on earth and un-der the earth, and every tongue acknowledge that Jesus Christ is Lord, to the glory of God the Father.[15]

Jesus is the example of what life with God looks like and his evaluation of prayer would suggest that public prayers full of well spoken words misses the mark. The statement at the end is the hard pill to swallow. Every day we seek to better ourselves. We want the better job, the nicer house, the fancier car, and the good life. We pursue the promotions and the vacations and the status symbols to let people know we are capable. We have pity on those who cannot

14. 1 Corinthians 11:1 NIV

15. Philippians 2:1–11 NIV

help themselves and pull ourselves up by our own hard efforts. This is also true in our life with God. We may feel like we communicate with God but never connect so we read books, go to seminars, go on silent retreats, and pray "without ceasing"—thinking that the hard effort will get us to our goal: life with God. To this Jesus says "if your righteousness does not surpass that of the Pharisees you will not enter the Kingdom of Heaven" but knowing the interactions captured in the four Gospel narratives between Jesus and the Pharisees I am not so sure they are the ones to mimic.

> To some who were confident of their own righteousness and looked down on everyone else, Jesus told this parable: "Two men went up to the temple to pray, one a Pharisee and the other a tax collector. The Pharisee stood by himself and prayed: 'God, I thank you that I am not like other people—robbers, evildoers, adulterers—or even like this tax collector. I fast twice a week and give a tenth of all I get.' "But the tax collector stood at a distance. He would not even look up to heaven, but beat his breast and said, 'God, have mercy on me, a sinner.' "I tell you that this man, rather than the other, went home justified before God. For all those who exalt themselves will be humbled, and those who humble themselves will be exalted."[16]

Listening to another person pray in public can be excruciating at times. I was in Phoenix for a visit with my aunt and uncle. It was a lazy afternoon, too hot to be outside, so we sat down to watch tv. My uncle asked if we had ever watched a NASCAR race, to which none of us responded yes. If you are a NASCAR fan, please excuse my critique of your hobby, but four hours—or more— of the same thing over and over got a little boring. I'm pretty sure even my uncle fell asleep during the race (granted I think he may already have known the outcome since this was a recorded race). Now I was not completely ignorant of NASCAR, I had seen the movie Talladega Knights with Will Ferrel. My favorite part is when he thinks he is on fire, but I digress. The movie has many humorous parts that I did not realize were actually rooted in NASCAR reality. The

16. Luke 18:9–14 NIV

racing, drinking, weird familial drama and the prayers. Will Ferrel constantly refers to Jesus as a baby, to the frustration of his wife. In there he also prays thanking God for his "smok'n hot wife" to which I thought "this movie is hilarious." My uncle cued up the NASCAR race and he said, "now some of the best part is right here at the beginning before the race, because they still have a prayer." Will Ferrel's prayers seemed tame compared to this actual guy, in front of national tv and thousands of people. He actually invoked the same "smok'n hot wife" comment. I think Will Ferrel still has the corner on praying to baby Jesus in swaddling clothes, but the portrayal of the somewhat ridiculous public prayers was actually on par for the reality of NASCAR. Have you been in that moment where someone stands up and prays and you wonder what in heaven and on earth is happening?

This reminds me of a friend whose father and grandfather were preachers. Whenever they would go out to eat, usually with church people or family, the grandfather would say the prayer for the food. On several vivid occasions my friend described the experience this way, "after the food was ordered grandpa would stand up at the head of the table in the restaurant and say a prayer. In a really loud voice, while standing, he would say 'God please help all these sinners be saved. . .' and we would all be so embarrassed." My dad actually grew up under the preaching of this friends grandpa. My dad described him as the sort of guy who would stop anyone in the grocery store and tell them the five steps of salvation. Do you ever feel embarrassed after you pray publicly? Jesus seems to be pretty critical of the "religious and righteous" guy's prayer in the parable he tells.

I was blessed to serve on the campus ministry team at Northwest Christian University my senior year. I was filling some big shoes of people who had really brought life and love to a growing student body exploring the call of God on our lives. My wife (future at the time) had been on the team the year before and I was excited to be mentored by our Campus Pastor and leave my mark on the school. The first thing our team did was go on a student life retreat with the other campus life teams. We did team building exercises, got to know the other teams we would be collaborating with, and spent time in prayer. In typical fashion we would open up our time in prayer and provide space for everyone who wanted to pray out loud and moments of silence as well. I was asked to close our teams prayer time in the afternoon near the end of the retreat. I finished and one of the more senior team leaders said "wow, I wish I could pray like that." To which I was completely caught off guard. It was in that moment that I realized just how much public prayer had become something I was "good" at. The next couple years my brother and I would reflect on just how much we judged people's depth and spiritual maturity on how they prayed. There were plenty of other variables but for us the one that seemed to matter the most and be the most consistent indicator was the persons prayer lingo and structure. Was I becoming the Pharisee rather than the tax collector?

The girl followed up her comment with some sort of invitation for me to teach her, and I am sure I mumbled something out that was unhelpful. The Campus Pastor stepped in, recognizing a teachable moment with the group. He said, "you know what is awesome about Lars when he prays? He always gets to the cross. No matter what he is praying about he brings it back to the cross." The conversation was redirected away from my prose, the word choices, the organization, the lack of clutter, or my own charisma; with the Campus Pastor's nudge toward the centrality of the cross. I learned as much from that interaction as I think the group did, in fact I would argue more. I now notice the times my prayers do not center on the cross. Public prayer is a great learning ground, but it is not something you perfect and achieve some status level of super spiritual maturity. In fact the problem with public prayer is the false maturity it seems to convey especially to yourself. Jesus' words following up his parable on prayer are "For all those who exalt themselves will be humbled, and those who humble themselves will be exalted."[17] Prayer is an invitation to humble yourself. Prayer is an opportunity for *humility* to produce fruit. Prayer at its core is not something you do publicly to grace others ears but an expression of *humility* before your abba, Father. This I believe is why Daniel

17. Jesus uses this exact phrase three different times. Matthew 23:12; Luke 14:11; Luke 18:14 NIV

prayed three times a day alone in his room rather than out in public places. This is why I believe Jesus tells us, in Matthew 6 moments before the famous example prayer is given, to "pray in secret and your father who is in secret will reward you." The instruction is even explicit: "go into your closet and close the door." Does this mean public prayer is wrong? No of course not. I would strongly argue for public prayer with narratives of the Old Testament and the birth of the Church in Acts. Our aim here is to consider life with God and the best example of that life is Jesus who makes a compelling argument for little public prayer. Jesus' longest prayer is recorded for us by the Apostle John, but tradition holds that this was only heard by his closest three companions in the heart of the garden of Gethsemane. It is hard to believe that this prayer was not somewhat formulated by John as it was written down so many years after the resurrection of Jesus, and so might more likely be a compilation of John and the other Apostles' recollections of that night and the week leading up to the crucifixion. With this in mind we would do right not to treat this as a public prayer but more of an example of the ongoing relationship and understanding between the Father and the Son. Jesus speaks of God's glory, of God's unity, and of God exalting Jesus because of his faithfulness to the mission. Prayer for Jesus in John 17 is a posture of *humility*.

Life with God, really knowing and being known by God as Jesus was and is, is a life of *humility*. Prayer is a demonstration of *humility* when it is less about words and images. Let us revisit the various relationships we discussed. The rather trite intimacy scale we used was marriage to fish with friendships and dogs in between. This scale is overly simplistic, yet the basics of it work for the discussion at hand. The posture of *humility* when God is the fish bowl on the kitchen counter seems ridiculous. It is one thing for a person to talk at the fish but listening for the fish to speak back would signal mental destabilization. How can one take a posture of humble listening when God is not expected to respond? The dog gets closer for we can place ourselves at the service of the nudges they non verbally communicate to us. Listening to what we infer the dog to be saying. This is an inexact science and often we put our own personality onto the dog. False humility is often demonstrated when we treat God this way. We attribute the nice and neat experiences to God's timing but refrain from wrestling with where the inferences are inconsistent with our own personality and judgement about who we think God is or should be. Human beings can talk back, so when God is treated as our friend or even best friend then we assume a lingo that sounds like a back and forth conversation. My more spirit-filled and charismatic friends adopt this posture often. They refer to agreements between them and God. They use phrases like "and God said" which is inspired by the way the Scriptural authors speak of God. But when you drill down to their experience most of what God has said to them is full of self noise. The words from God are amidst a flurry of their own self talk, whether it was vivid dreams, visions, words from wise and trusted mentors, Scripture, or other inner voices. The person cannot usually slow down long enough to explain one word from God before steam rolling ahead to the next thing they feel. They talk about the words from God using the same language as when talking to themselves or thinking about a situation. God could be eliminated from their sentences and what they said would sound like someone who just has an overly active self processor. These are broad strokes and generalities from many different kinds of conversations with people. I realize I do the same thing many times when I try to convince myself that something is God's will and plan for my life. I look for evidence that I can point to, through friends and Scripture reading to back up the feeling I have within me. I am just not as practiced in the language codex they have for naming it as the move of God in my life. The catch is interpreting when it is God and when it is my over active brain. Do you ever find yourself thinking like one of my youth group student's "so prayer is like a text message, except God never replies?"

Marriage is the next step on the relational scale. I believe that God created the human experience of marriage and specifically the biological nature of reproduction the way it is, namely physical sexual intercourse, as something that points to the intimacy, knowing, the Triune God exists in. God desires for us to be united with the Triune God head. This is why Paul calls sex a great mystery while also calling the mysterious hope God planned from the beginning was Christ in you. The depth and quality of your life with God is not determined by your marital status, your desire to or not to get married, gender, or orientation. I use marriage not to elevate its place in society but because it is so foundational to the human experience. We are sexual beings and like it or not we exist and continue to exist as a species because of sex. A posture of *humility* in a marriage, especially when it comes to sex, is—at its core—listening. In premarital counseling you are asked to have a conversation with your partner about the sexual expectations you each have. Whether you want children, and if so, how many is often part of this discussion. Later, in marriage, the conversations get a bit more practical. The problem is not asking what you can do to meet your partner's needs but really listening in the moment of passion. Listening not just for words but the joys and invitations of your partner. The posture of *humility* means you have to quiet your own desires, empty your expectations, and listen. To truly know and be known by God we have to quiet ourselves, our expectations, and especially our bodies (words, voices, thinking, and desires) long enough to be drawn with the invitations and joys of God. This is spiritual maturity, this is the prayer life of Jesus, this is eternal life, this is life with God. The next three chapters speak to my understanding of how to cultivate and form this life with God centered around three virtues: *humility*, *gratitude*, and *simplicity*.

Chapter 2

Humility: The Way of Listening

NOW: WHAT IS HAPPENING NOW? | CAR RIDES AND ARGUMENTS

I remember vividly one day when Janel and I were driving in the car together. The traffic was heavy so we knew we were in for a long one, not an uncommon experience for those of us who live in Los Angeles. The conversation began about the work I do with students merely because I could not think of something better to talk about. Now do not get me wrong, I am passionate about my work (often so passionate it is all we talk about), but I try to vary the topic of conversation so that Janel is not bored. Needless to say I had failed once again to move the subject matter. As the conversation died down I mentioned a crazy hair-brained idea I had regarding bi-vocational ministry, something my wife hears me wax eloquently about every few days. It began with the normal rose colored lenses common to grass is greener brainstorming: "oh it would be so different if I was only working part time at the church and teaching too. . .I mean a private school would probably be the best. . .I mean at least then I would be with students every day making an actual difference in their lives. . ." This is where the conversation took a nasty turn.

My wife is a teacher, she has her teaching credential for elementary (multiple subject) and has taught middle school and substituted in high school. She is also the head volleyball coach at a very difficult and low income public high school in Pasadena. She responded to my rant by addressing my complaint about attendance issues because my students are not required to come (there are some days I wish the entrance to heaven included an attendance requirement, sure would get those students to youth group). She pointed out that if I was teaching every day, even a Bible class at a private school, does not mean the students will actually learn or appreciate what I do. She was simply giving me some practical, real life perspective to keep my brainstorming grounded in reality. What happened next was my least favorite of the arguments we have had in the past year. I countered every point by grumbling more and more about my current job. The argument ended with my wife saying "well then maybe you should not do ministry." The observation hurt because I know this is my calling and passion, I know this is where God wants me and what my healthy self lives for; but you see my healthy self wasn't the one arguing.

Humility was what I lacked in the car that day. I wanted to be right so badly I was willing to say just about anything, including contradicting myself just to win a point. I was like a lawyer so hell bent on winning that I was willing to submit false evidence to just beat the other side. What was worse was that in this situation the other side was my wife, who I am deeply committed to and connected with. However that day, I allowed my pride to cause conflict and disconnection.

Humility is sustained through *gratitude*. When we are thankful, we spend less time thinking about what we do not have. Thankfulness for the other person leads to and is the outpouring of *humility*. My father often says "sometimes you can think your way into a better way of acting, but a lot of the time you act your way into a better way of thinking." Being thankful is the action that leads to *humility*. If I had been thankful for my wife's sound advice, and especially thankful for her work as an experienced teacher, I would not have been so focused on being "right" and winning the argument.

Driving is a great test of *humility*. "Merge, everybody merge. . ." Brian Regan says in one of his comedy routines and gets a bunch of laughs because it is true. We have this burst of adrenaline when entering a freeway or at a four way stop. "It is my turn now, thank you very much!" Hopefully we just mutter under our breath that and the other not so pleasantries. Road rage, at least in LA, is a real thing. Even many godly friends and mentors of mine lament about the traffic when they come to visit LA. And those who live here seem to erode with every hour they spend in bumper to bumper traffic. Getting cut off, letting someone else go ahead of you, or even the way in which you merge can be a small test of *humility* each day. What might it look like for you to be thankful for the person in front of you or the one who cut you off? Both of you are safe and alive by God's grace. What value does it add to your life to flip the other driver off and utter negativity into your own car and the lives of those with you? *Humility* is not only to be practiced with those closest to us —with our spouse, at church, those we work with—*humility* is a virtue, an essential part of our everyday lives. *Humility* is best observed in the mundane of every day moments because we act out of our conditioned habits during the catastrophic events of life.

KNOW: WHAT DO WE KNOW ABOUT GOD? | JESUS AS THE EXAMPLE

Jesus continues speaking of the Kingdom of God (or Heaven in Matthew's account) throughout his whole life and ministry. So much so that the twelve disciples begin arguing about who is the greatest in this kingdom. They finally muster the courage to ask:

> At that time the disciples came to Jesus and asked, "Who, then, is the greatest in the kingdom of heaven?" He called a little child to him, and placed the child among them. And he said: "Truly I tell you, unless you change and become like little children, you will never enter the kingdom of heaven. Therefore, whoever takes the lowly

position of this child is the greatest in the kingdom of heaven. And whoever welcomes one such child in my name welcomes me.[1]

Becoming like Jesus means becoming humble, and becoming humble according to Jesus is to become like a child. What does Jesus mean by this visual lesson? Well, the child would have been smaller than all these men. The disciples were likely in their early twenties or late teens. Since I am in my late twenties, I can resonate with what was likely true for these twelve guys: I can do anything, I am invincible, I will change the world! Jesus comes and says, psych, that is the wrong playbook. Being great in this kingdom does not involve changing the world (at least not in the way we think) or the power you think you have. No, the greatness comes from taking a lowly position of a child. Jesus even acknowledges that a child is lowly. Before you go and think I am discounting Jesus' liberation teaching and inclusion of the outcast—I want you to notice Jesus' point here is *humility*.

Humility is setting aside your self. Jesus is inviting the disciples (and us!) to set aside all of their control, power, status, strength, and independence to become dependent on God. We must become like little children who come with nothing to offer, nothing to trade, nothing to barter, no way to leverage, no bribe or coercion technique. *Humility* means we come to God and others with no agendas for our own betterment.

> On one occasion an expert in the law stood up to test Jesus. "Teacher," he asked, "what must I do to inherit eternal life?"
>
> "What is written in the Law?" he replied. "How do you read it?"
>
> He answered, "'Love the Lord your God with all your heart and with all your soul and with all your strength and with all your mind'; and, 'Love your neighbor as yourself.'"
>
> "You have answered correctly," Jesus replied. "Do this and you will live."

1. Matthew 18:1-5 NIV

But he wanted to justify himself, so he asked Jesus, "And who is my neighbor?"

In reply Jesus said: "A man was going down from Jerusalem to Jericho, when he was attacked by robbers. They stripped him of his clothes, beat him and went away, leaving him half dead. A priest happened to be going down the same road, and when he saw the man, he passed by on the other side. So too, a Levite, when he came to the place and saw him, passed by on the other side. But a Samaritan, as he traveled, came where the man was; and when he saw him, he took pity on him. He went to him and bandaged his wounds, pouring on oil and wine. Then he put the man on his own donkey, brought him to an inn and took care of him. The next day he took out two denarii and gave them to the innkeeper. 'Look after him,' he said, 'and when I return, I will reimburse you for any extra expense you may have.'

"Which of these three do you think was a neighbor to the man who fell into the hands of robbers?"

The expert in the law replied, "The one who had mercy on him."

Jesus told him, "Go and do likewise."[2]

I was fourteen years old when I was living with my family in Vietnam. The pastor at our church had previously worked in Cambodia and still wanted to help that area, so we gathered a group to do a short term missions trip from Vietnam to Cambodia via bus. The experience was not unlike ones I had in Vietnam of working with orphanages, having interpreters, and being hot all the time. The unique part was the team we were serving with. We prepared several months in advance for our week long trip. The pastor challenged several of us to share our testimonies and lead a drama. Several in our group opted to do a dance with choreography depicting Jesus' death, burial, and resurrection. I decided to help direct a skit of the "Good Samaritan." My brother rode his unicycle as the man going down from Jerusalem to Jericho, he was attacked by squirt gun wielding robbers, and carried on the back of a mask wearing high school senior pretending to be a donkey. I was privileged to

2. Luke 10:25–37 NIV

introduce the story and narrate alongside the interpreter. We shared this story with several orphanages near Phnom Penh but I think the experience left a longer lasting effect on me than on any of the orphans. Sure they laughed hard at the unicycle and pretend donkey, but Jesus' words "go and do likewise" continue to gnaw at me.

What is Jesus actually asking of us in this passage? Take pity on others? Bind up their wounds? We have the Red Cross, social services, EMT's, and hospitals that provide medical care much better than I ever could. The attitude of the heart, to have mercy on others, seems to be what Jesus responds to. The story begins with an action question "what must I do to inherit eternal life?" Then we hear about the people who do not show mercy. These holy men are actually the ones who should have the attitude of heart most attune to the love of God. Jesus over and over points out those who are true followers "[do] the will of my Father in Heaven" which is to "hear these words of mine and puts them into practice."[3]. The priest and the Levite know God's law better than the Samaritan. Their lives are ordered around honoring God. They are both set apart, holy if you will, for this purpose. But many infer from Jesus' story that the priest and Levite most likely avoided the man because of potential uncleanness. This would have affected them because, had they contracted any uncleanness from the man, they would have no longer been allowed to serve their duty post at the Temple or in their village. Coming in contact with a dead body or bodily fluids would require extra time and effort to repeat ceremonial cleansing rituals in order to serve. *Humility* puts into practice mercy. Our needs and our roles are not more important than becoming present to and attending to the needs of others. My position and my responsibilities are not so important that passing by those in need just to be productive and efficient is okay.

Genuine *humility* is not a status you receive, it is a lifestyle you cultivate. As a full time youth worker I often get accolades from others about just how important my work is. However, the person commenting often has no real sense of what I do on a daily basis. They assume and project an air of awe that at times feels very

---

3. Matthew 7:21, 24 NIV

disingenuous. Why does this bother me? Well it bothers me because I want it to be true, but I am deeply aware of the times and ways in which I do not live up to the narrative they just laid out. I believe the same goes for *humility*. One might be considered humble because you are not wealthy or famous, but that does not equate to actually being humble. Most of the people I know who need to work on their *humility* are the least well known or networked people in my circles. I have also had the privilege of meeting many of my heroes who have tremendous influence and are famous (at least to me) that are incredibly humble. *Humility* is not something you just naturally do, it is something you cultivate and grow inside you. The priest and the Levite knew a lot about mercy, but they were not in the habit of practicing mercy; otherwise they would not have passed by. The Samaritan may not have had a systematic theology of mercy but he was in the habit of practicing mercy. It is the everyday moments that develop and cultivate *humility*, patterns of practice rather than status. This is why the prophet proclaims:

> He has shown you, O mortal, what is good.
> And what does the Lord require of you?
> To act justly and to love mercy
> and to walk humbly with your God.[4]

But why is it so rare to come across authentic *humility*? Perhaps we have become numb to the idea of *humility* because we are so accustomed to false *humility*. What is true *humility* and how does one cultivate it?

Several key stories in the Old Testament demonstrate the separation from God and destruction that comes from pride and seeking our betterment over others. *Humility* is demonstrated by a laying down of power, authority, control, ego, and self. This is achieved through a healthy understanding of self importance, or what the Apostle Paul says "thinking of ourselves in sober judgement."[5] The prophet Isaiah speaks of the humble suffering servant of God; a foreshadowing of Jesus the ultimate example. The Apostle Paul keys in on this humble, suffering, servant motif in his

4. Micah 6:8 NIV

5. Romans 12:3 NIV

letter to the Philippians: "[Jesus] being in very nature God, did not consider equality with God something to be grasped but humbled himself and became obedient to death, even death on the cross."[6]

Humility does not lead to prosperity, humility leads to the cross. It is not the cross that is to be celebrated it is the *humility* Jesus shows to come and live as we are, and further to die. Reading Scripture then becomes an act of *humility*, an act of becoming like Jesus in our own dying. Jonah is an example of doing all the right religion (bringing the message of God to the world) but missing *humility* and so living miserably though seemingly having everything he could have ever wanted. Becoming like Jesus does not always lead where we think it will. In fact many people read the Bible, sing worship songs a few Sundays a month, are members of a church, and yet struggle to be humble in the most ordinary ways. Why does *humility* escape our grasp?

"Imitate me as I imitate Christ."[7] These words from the Apostle Paul might sound a bit high and mighty. Who does Paul think he is? But this is discipleship, we are to emulate and imitate those around us who are further along on the journey of becoming more like Jesus. It makes sense for Paul to use language like Philippians 4:9, "and whatever you have heard from me or seen in me put it into practice and the God of peace will be with you." A strong claim, but Paul is merely following in a pattern he knew well from the priestly tradition. God gave Aaron and his sons a blessing to pronounce on the people: "and when you bless the people say 'The Lord bless you and keep you. The Lord make his face to shine upon you and be gracious to you. The Lord turn his face toward you and give you peace.' So you will place my name upon them and I will bless them."[8] The priests had to have a healthy understanding of who they were as God's instruments of blessing, and it was through their blessing that God gave peace. *Humility* results in peace.

Jesus came preaching a message of repentance because the kingdom of God was near. Repentance is about changing our minds,

6. Philippians 2:6 NIV

7. 1 Corinthians 11:1 NIV

8. Numbers 6:22–27 NIV

or mental models, the way we see and envision the world. *Humility* means changing how we see and make value judgements about others. *Humility* changes what is important to us. *Humility* causes us to die to ourselves so that others might experience God's peace. *Humility* centers around the Shema. Shema is the Hebrew word for "hear" and is the shortened title for "Shema Israel" or "hear, O Israel" the opening words for the great commandment. When asked what the greatest commandment is, Jesus sums the whole of the Old Testament revelation of God into these words: "Love the Lord your God with all your heart, soul, mind, and strength and love your neighbor as yourself."[9] The Golden rule flows from a similar teaching of Jesus' when he says "do to others as you would have them do to you."[10] Genuine *humility* comes from a place of health: love of God and love of self. Jesus embodies this *humility* the night he was betrayed when he prays on the Mount of Olives: "Father, if you are willing, take this cup (*suffering and death on behalf of others*) from me (*healthy love of self*); yet not my will (*setting aside self*), but yours be done (*love of God*)."[11]

Let's take a closer look at the beautiful recalling of the Gospel by the Apostle Paul in Philippians 2.

> In your relationships with one another, have the same mindset as Christ Jesus:
> Who, being in very nature God, did not consider equality with God something to be used to his own advantage; rather, he made himself nothing by taking the very nature of a servant, being made in human likeness. And being found in appearance as a man, he humbled himself by becoming obedient to death—even death on a cross! Therefore God exalted him to the highest place and gave him the name that is above every name, that at the name of Jesus every knee should bow, in heaven and on earth and under the earth, and every tongue acknowledge that Jesus Christ is Lord, to the glory of God the Father.[12]

9. Matthew 22:34–40 NIV
10. Matthew 7:12 NIV
11. Luke 22:42 NIV emphasis mine.
12. Philippians 2:5–11 NIV

The core of the Christian message is contained these poetic lines. Many scholars attribute it to an early Christian hymn familiar to Paul's readers. He weaves this song within the letter much like a preacher today will draw upon the hymn "Amazing Grace" or the Apostles Creed. The love Paul has for the Philippians is all over this small letter. The opening of chapter two seems to be where Paul is saying, "If my love has provided you with any consolation in your suffering...then please now respond properly to my request."[13] Paul writes them an urgent request from what Gerald Hawthorne calls "the deepest experiences common to every Christian —encouragement in Christ, incentive of love, fellowship of the Spirit, tenderness and compassion."[14] His desire is for unity which is expressed at length in 1 Corinthians 1 and Ephesians 4. We all know unity is important, but we still find ourselves living divided. At the time of this writing, racism and political division are at heightened states as the first term of President Donald Trump nears a close and things do not look to be getting better. So is Paul just another pie in the sky by and by Christian who says "unity is at the heart of the Gospel," and leaves us scratching our heads at what to do next? No, instead Paul's appeal is incredibly practical. Unity is an outpouring of *humility* and "self sacrifice flows from a willingness to restrain one's own desire in order to satisfy the desires of others."[15] The problem is we have been duped too many times by false unity. Welcomed in only to stabbed in the back or ostracized by the very ones who opened the door into the group. We begin to doubt real and lasting unity could ever exist. We encounter failed moments of connection with the people who can quote biblical truth, but who are often using the church for their own personal power and privilege. I was just reading on Facebook a post where a Christian mused about the tragedy that so many people leave church because of relationships. What this Christian did not name, but I believe Paul does is that too many Christians are not humble. Paul is inviting these saved people, who have benefited tremendously from the saving work of

13. Hawthorne. *Philippians*. 65

14. Ibid., 64

15. Ibid., 64

Jesus and the relationships found in the church, to embrace a life of *humility*. The real work of unity is *humility* experienced at the broad society level and cultivated within by individuals.

DO: WHAT SHOULD WE TRY TO DO? | HUMILITY PRACTICES

So what should we try to do about incorporating *humility* into our life? I believe a well rounded approach to learning to listen to God involves learning to listen to other people in our life. The ones we actually interact with every day, online, in coffee shops, on the road, and in our neighborhoods. Let's start with some practices of listening to other people and then we'll look at some specific prayer practices that can help us listen for God's voice.

Listening to Other People

This probably goes in the common sense category, but I believe listening is a learned practice. Practice makes perfect, or I should say "perfect" practice makes perfect. How can we expect to listen to God if we do not listen to other people we can see? Here are five ways I've practiced listening to people:

Stories.

Build in regular times where you listen to people's stories. Schedule and block out enough time to go beyond the highlights. Our church has cultivated story-telling as part of their mentoring groups and young adult ministry, and we've seen the benefits from story-telling resulting in deeper relationships.

Restaurants.

I mentioned in the introduction a new practice I have tried to cultivate by asking the person taking my order what they recommend.

If you're feeling adventurous, this might be a meaningful practice in your own life. Doing so frees up your mind to dig into deeper conversation with your companions. You can also use time at restaurants to listen to what foods your friends are passionate about and enjoy eating. All around, time at restaurants can be enlightening for you and can be a great space for you to engage in meaningful conversation.

Questions.

Asking good questions is actually more difficult than you might think. A thoughtful question requires active listening and pause before speaking. I am not advising you to be a busy body that pries into everyone's business all the time; rather I am suggesting you do your best to slow down and lean into more intimate conversation. Open ended questions or phrases like "tell me more" or "I'm curious what that was like" are helpful practices. If you are like me, you manage conversations. Try to let it meander rather than managing and directing the conversation toward a goal.

Silence.

I strongly suggest spending time in silence. If you're an introvert you're probably happy to hear this suggestion. But hear me out, extroverts, I'm not trying to permanently silence you! The invitation to spending time in silence is to practice, primarily with people you know well, cultivating time together that requires fewer words. This doesn't mean mindlessly watching TV, scrolling your phone, or being "alone together." I'm suggesting that you spend time noticing the non verbal communication and allowing dead space every once in a while. If you're the talkative one in the relationship, take a step back by allowing others to lead conversation. If you're the quiet one, this practice can lead you you to engage more actively and model healthy listening.

Reading aloud.

This is likely the hardest of the five suggestions to implement because we have very few outlets for this. The Bible tells us about a practice kings used when they had trouble falling asleep. They would have the minutes or records of their kingdom read aloud. Now this may have been because only a small portion of people were able to read and write. When Moses receives the ten commandments he gathers everyone together and reads aloud the instructions to them. The oral tradition of storytelling was actually how much of our Bible and the teachings of Jesus were passed down for years before someone who had the ability collected the oral traditions and wrote them down. The epistles or letters of Paul like Romans and Ephesians were actually meant to be read aloud in the gathering of Christians. Paul's little house churches would receive a letter and someone would read it out loud to everyone. I believe our culture has become very focused on the individual, we do our own personal study and reading. Listening to others read aloud or reading aloud to others promotes a common experience. Church is a great place to promote this public reading. Since many of the stories in the Bible were originally passed down as oral traditions, reading it aloud often becomes more meaningful than just reading silently on our own. I would encourage you to find people in your life who will read the Bible aloud with you. I know there are other ways from reading a short devotional book together with your spouse, a bedtime story for your kids, or a book club with friends. I would love to hear about the creative ways you are cultivating listening.

These five invitations to listen become opportunities to notice the Spirit of God at work in your ordinary moments. As you listen to someone telling their story, how are you encountering the triune God in what unfolds? At the restaurants you frequent do you see the face of Christ, the image of God, in the servers? Asking good questions can be a way of exercising and noticing your own image of God creativity at work through curiosity. As you become more comfortable with silence in the presence of others you will find meaning in the silent moments with the great Other, God. And reading aloud I believe connects us to God's wisdom and knowledge. This may seem like a stretch, but I believe the Bible connects us not only with those we are with today but Christians throughout the generations who have read this book. So also we are connected to God by reading. As we read aloud the Prophets who speak for God or the red lettered passages of Jesus in the Gospels, we are hearing aloud the very words of God. As we cultivate listening habits with other people we are conditioning our hearts to be humble.

Breathing as Listening

Mindfulness has become very popular, but I am not just bandwagoning here. There really is something to it. In fact scientists have done experiments on rats to prove that deep breathing does in fact calm and reduce anxiety. Yoga and new applications like CALM which you can find on your smart phone or even Apple TV, help us create space to be in touch with our feelings through breathing. Many prayer practices incorporate breathing as well. The same concept of creating space is at play. This is why breathing can be a good way to begin to listen more closely for God's voice. These are three prayer practices that involve breathing I've incorporated into my life:

Prayer of Examen by St. Ignatius.

This is meant to be done at the end of the day or week as a reflective practice. It encourages reviewing past time in thankfulness, as well as taking notice to both positive and negative feelings you've felt. Finally, you're prompted to speak with the Lord about those feelings and look forward to the day or week ahead with hope. All done while breathing deeply and slowly.

Breath Prayer.

This is a practice in which you choose a word or phrase to root you in your prayer. One word or phrase takes you through your inhale while another takes you through the exhale. An example that's been meaningful to me is: "I am here" on the inhale and "You are here" on the exhale.

Breathing and Bible Reading.

If you have a Bible reading plan already in place, great! If not, starting small with a Psalm a day would be a great place to start. A powerful way to engage with this practice can look something like this:

> Psalm 42:1–2,11 NIV
>
> (inhale) As the deer pants for streams of water,
> (exhale) so my soul pants for you, my God.
> (inhale) My soul thirsts for God,
> (exhale) for the living God.
> (inhale) When can I go and meet with God?
> (exhale) Why, my soul, are you downcast?
> (inhale) Why so disturbed within me?
> (exhale) Put your hope in God,
> (inhale) for I will yet praise him,
> (exhale) my Savior and my God.

Creating space to be conscious and in touch with our feelings is what breathing helps us do. Instead of being reactive and chaotic, we are able to know ourselves and be in touch with those around us so we are calm and present. The same goes with God. When we quiet our anxious and chaotic thoughts we are able to listen and allow God to do God's business of transforming our hearts.

Humility Needs Gratitude

Humility may be the pathway to know God, to truly listen and pay attention to God's presence in our lives, but it is not easy. We need ways to sustain a life of *humility* and not fall prey to false *humility* and humiliation. This is why we must consider *gratitude* along with *humility*. Being thankful is how we put on the new lenses and sustain seeing the world through the correct lens of *humility*. We may find ourselves humbled and in heightened awareness of God's closeness because of a life circumstance or event. Perhaps in the joy brought by the birth of a child we are humbled. Or we are humbled in the tragedy of the loss of a dear friend or loved one. At the mountaintops or ocean shores we are humbled by the overwhelming awe of the power of the Spirit of God. But these are only brief momentary retreats in our often hectic and overly busy lives. We need to be grounded in the constant presence of the Spirit of Christ in us during both the extraordinary and ordinary; we need *gratitude*.

Chapter 3

Gratitude: The Way of Being

NOW: WHAT IS HAPPENING NOW? | THE PRESENT

The Tonight Show has always had iconic hosts. The current host, Jimmy Fallon, has continued to make a mark on comedy. A signature of his show is a bit called "Thank You Notes." The crowd rolls in laughter as celebrities are thanked for hilarious and often strange things they do. I remember being at summer camp and enjoying some good jokes via the "thank you notes" comedy. I could tell you several from camp but they would fall flat in this medium. Why? Because, as the old adage goes, "you had to be there." The comedic magic of the "Thank you Notes" is their attentiveness to the present. We all have experienced the feeling of cluelessness in the eyes of someone we are trying to repeat a great joke or funny experience to. When they do not react how we had hoped, we try and coverup the awkwardness with "I guess you had to be there." With the invention of the camera, we now can capture the moment and relive it. This is great for those of us who love to watch re-runs of our favorite *Friends* episode or home movies of when we were kids, but this is a relatively recent development in human history. Cave paintings, Egyptian hieroglyphics, and other ways of telling history in the past were interpretations and stories. Now we have live news, Facebook live, livestream, and YouTube that show us exactly what happened and are not mediated. We record our kids' recitals, their first words, our friends stupidest moment—so many of us live the present through a screen saying "it's all good, I can just go back and watch that later." The practice of gratitude challenges our flippant dismissal of the present, inviting us to avoid the trap of living in the past or the future, and instead embrace the present.

KNOW: WHAT DO WE KNOW ABOUT GOD? | GOODNESS AND LOVE

"Let the peace of Christ rule in your hearts since as members of one body you were called to peace. And be thankful. . ."[1] Amidst a passage containing lots of big concepts Paul drops in reminders to be thankful. He seems to value *gratitude* very much because he closes this section with a command to do everything in the Name of Jesus, and it is almost like he says "oh and give thanks to God through Jesus." If you grew up in a Christian home like me, you probably said "Grace" or prayed (or as our cook in Vietnam would say, "talk over your food") which we find Jesus calling "giving thanks." Prayer is fundamentally a way of expressing our thanks to God. But saying "thanks" three times a day seems to miss some of what Paul seems to be getting at in Colossians 3. *Gratitude* is a way of life.

> Shout for joy to the Lord, all the earth. Worship the Lord with gladness; come before him with joyful songs. Know that the Lord is God. It is he who made us, and we are his; we are his people, the sheep of his pasture. Enter his gates with thanksgiving and his courts with praise; give thanks to him and praise his name. For the Lord is good and his love endures forever; his faithfulness continues through all generations.[2]

1. Colossians 3:15 NIV
2. Psalm 100 NIV

This familiar call to worship, which you may hear read on a Sunday, is full of rich imagery. *Gratitude* is not just a "please and thank you" etiquette for dinner parties or being polite to dignitaries. *Gratitude* to the Yahweh, the LORD, is full of shouting and joy. The exuberant giving of thanks covers every part of life. First in the acknowledgement of our coming into existence is due to God, so we thank God for making us! Second, the psalmist notes God's relationship to us. God is like our parent, we are the kiddos—siblings in Christ. Like a shepherd caring for sheep, we are under God's protection and care. We belong to the Lord. Third, there is mention of gates and courts. The presence of God is open to us through Jesus. The psalmist writes envisioning a temple that had physical gates and courts, all with significance and meaning. In Jesus the gate is open and we are welcomed into the court of God. I remember our trip to Washington D.C. in 2007. A coworker of my dad connected us with a representative from Congress who got us a tour of the White House and a private tour of the Capitol building. The representative's aid took us to the floor of the House while they were out of session and we got to sit where the Supreme Court justices sit during the State of the Union addresses. Courts, justice, and government are all things we often separate from religion. But in the Bible, the people of God were a nation with a government and God was their king (up until the time of King Saul). The psalmist is reminding us to come to God for justice, to trust God as our king and to be grateful for God's rule in our life. Fourth and finally, our song of *gratitude* ends with a reminder of God's love for us which is linked to God's goodness and faithfulness. How do we know that God is loving? How do we know God is good? How do we know God is faithful and someone worth trusting? Psalm 136 and others recount historical events in Israel's history to point out how God has shown love, goodness, and faithfulness. The poem has the repeated refrain: "his love endures forever."[3] Do you know the stories of God's love in your history, your family, your life? Are you telling these stories through song, poetry, narrative, testimony? During my time at Fuller Seminary I was invited to write my own psalm. This was a powerful practice of reflection for me, and I encourage you to do the same. You may not be a writer, and poetry or lyrics may not be the best

3. Psalm 136

medium for you to express your thoughts. But finding ways to tell the story of God's love in your life will help you remember and share with others the witness of God's power in your life.

> [12] As Jesus was going into a village, ten men who had leprosy met him. They stood at a distance [13] and called out in a loud voice, "Jesus, Master, have pity on us!" 14 When he saw them, he said, "Go, show yourselves to the priests." And as they went, they were cleansed. [15] One of them, when he saw he was healed, came back, praising God in a loud voice. [16] He threw himself at Jesus' feet and thanked him—and he was a Samaritan. [17] Jesus asked, "Were not all ten cleansed? Where are the other nine? [18] Has no one returned to give praise to God except this foreigner?" [19] Then he said to him, "Rise and go; your faith has made you well."[4]

I find this story fascinating because all of the lepers were healed, all trusted Jesus and did what he said to do. The Samaritan is actually the one who disobeyed in some ways. Jesus said to go to the priest, but he was overcome with *gratitude* so he made a choice to return to Jesus instead of going to show himself to the priest. Being grateful is more visceral and powerful than just obedience. The other nine were healed, the other nine were obedient, but the other nine were not thankful. There are lots of moments when we are healed, there are lots of times when we obey, but when was the last time you really stopped following everyone else and instead "returned" to the feet of Jesus to offer your thanks? Okay, I have never had the experience of leprosy, and I have never been miraculously healed by Jesus. Luke, the Gospel writer who recounts this encounter, includes this story here I think because of the note regarding the nationality of the one who returned. You see, Jesus' question identifies the point of the story "where are the other nine?" As someone who has grown up Christian I can become complacent and expect God to show up and heal. I can take for granted what God is doing in my life. I can miss out on the revelatory moments when the Holy Spirit makes Jesus known to me. The Samaritan in this story

---

4. Luke 17:12–19 NIV

does not take for granted the healing experience, instead he ignores the "ritual" and returns to Jesus. They needed to present themselves clean and healed to the priest in order to be reintegrated to society and their families. Otherwise they legally were required to remain separate and outside the towns. But the Samaritan is so overcome with *gratitude* that the first thing he does is thank Jesus. *Gratitude* is not a "logical" or "calculated" decision, it is a rash one. I imagine as they looked down at their skin because the itching or oozing had stopped, one by one they began to pick up their pace running faster toward the priest, toward their freedom from this life of being the outcast. But as they all started dreaming about what they would do first (pick up their children, hug their parents, kiss their wives, have dinner with friends..), the Samaritan stopped and turned 180 degrees to head back towards Jesus shouting at the top of his lungs with joy and *gratitude*. When was the last time you made a scene about being grateful to God?

Gratitude has been called a "parent virtue" that, like a mother, gives birth to other virtues like kindness and patience. If *humility* is the pathway to authentic relationship with God, *gratitude* is what sustains *humility*. One of the dark sides of *humility* is humiliation. Without *gratitude* sustaining our life, we can veer off into self deprecating humor, dark self criticism, and martyrdom. *Gratitude* grounds us in the present reality of the goodness of God, creation, the breath of life, the spirit of creativity, community, and our own limitations. This is freedom from the dark sides of *humility*, freedom found in the little moments of right now. Another shadow of *humility* can be expressed in cynicism. Practices of thankfulness require positivity to counter hardness gathering on our hearts through disappointments and the emptying of ourselves.

The hearty "belly laugh" or the deep "tearful laughing" that comes from really great comedy is actually good for your soul according to research on how the body, mind, and emotions work. We receive positive endorphins released into our body when we laugh so fully. Our mind is cleared and refreshed with positivity and hopefulness. Our emotions relax from anxiety and fear, and we are more likely to pursue intimacy with others in moments of laughter. This is because in those moments of laughter we are truly present to our mind, body, and emotions in a unique way. The same is true of *gratitude*. When we review our day and our lives in thanksgiving we enter into an awareness and centeredness that is not common in our frantic and frenetic paced lives. We drive faster and farther in crowded traffic in over populated cities. We look at pictures and posts on our phones while watching shows on our tv, bombarded by ads that tell us we need more things. So we work longer hours to buy the things we want, in order to watch more tv and in turn want more which means we must work more. And so the vicious cycle continues. You may relate or you may not, but the ache inside of each of us is there because we have all "[fallen] short of the glory of God."[5]

I used to think of God's glory as being a picture of light shining out of the clouds. God's glory was for me like greek mythology surrounding Zeus' powerful lightning. God was this European strong man with a great white beard wielding powerful bolts of light and coming on the clouds. Not too dissimilar from Anthony Hopkins as the Norse god Odin in the recent Marvel films. Now this image of God is not entirely absent in the Hebrew Scriptures (the storm god part, not the white beard). There is the mountain of God where God passes by Moses in Exodus 33 and Moses gets to see God's back. There is also an encounter with the people of Israel at this mountain where thunder and lightning so frighten them that they ask Moses to go speak with God "otherwise we will surely die." But all of these expressions of God's glory are mediated—communicated to us via metaphor, story, word pictures, and historical accounts of miraculous encounters—through the human experience. We cannot forget the humanness of the Hebrew and Christian Scriptures when we come to the interpretation of things like God's glory. Word pictures, just like paintings and modern photography are visuals that capture an angle. New 3D cameras draw us into a multiple perspective, but even 4D experiences are incapable of capturing everything. I recently went through a virtual reality (VR) experience called "The Void" at Downtown Disney in Anaheim, CA. We completed a mission together that involved walking through doorways, picking up

---

5. Romans 3:23 NIV

weapons, riding elevators, and fighting off stormtroopers in this Star Wars themed VR. I wonder how long it will be before we begin to have historic VR's, where we can go back and walk with Jesus to Golgotha, or Moses through the Red Sea. Still, these will be mediated experiences, unlike the present. If we imagine God's glory as synonymous with the mediated and interpreted expressions found in the Scriptures, we can end up with the wrong expectations for how God will show up in our lives. This is why *gratitude* is what sustains a life of knowing God. We need *humility* to listen and enter in a relationship with God, and we need gratitude to sustain that life. God's glory is God's presence in the present. The wilderness wandering was a formational period of time in Israel's history. God was teaching them *humility* (how to be in relationship with God) but they did not enter the promised land the first time they arrived at the Jordan because they lived out of fear instead of responding to God's glory and presence with *gratitude*. Many of the psalms teach us how *gratitude* can shape generations. When we practice *gratitude* it continually reminds us of God's glory and presence among us. When we are ungrateful we tend to live in fear which is counter to the way of the life God desires for us.

At the foot of the mountain, the people of Israel feared the Lord's presence (the glory of God expressed in clouds of thunder and lightning). Instead of being humble enough to come before God's presence and lay down their own control, they missed out on direct communication with God. They were humbled leaving Egypt by God's power and presence, but even in the short moments following their Exodus they respond ungratefully. I could have written these chapters on *Humility*, *Gratitude*, and *Simplicity* in any order, for to see them as a progression is missing the intricacies of how interwoven they are. It might be better to express them through the visual of a snail's shell. The spiraling effects cause one to see progression as a continuous yet always moving inward process that has no beginning and no end. Think of it like a cycle back and forth as one learns *humility* focus shifts (like this book does) onto *gratitude* but in learning *gratitude* one returns again to *humility* to learn the lessons deeper as new doorways open for further understanding of these key virtues. As one learns to humble themselves before

God, new reasons and opportunities for *gratitude* and thankfulness arise—around and down we go, spiraling further into knowing God.

The presence of God is not just in the lightning but in the every day moments. As an amateur scholar I spend too much time in the world of the mind. I read, re-read, and study historic events and muse over the future. This is why *gratitude* is so critical. If God's presence (glory) is not just something in the past or awaiting me in the future (as some teach that God's glory resides only in a heavenly after life) then I need a way of grounding myself in today, in God's glory right now. At this Starbucks where I am writing, God's glory is in the barista's creativity, the children with their parents, the smiles on faces as caffeine is consumed, and energy of the Spirit as it fills all things at all times. But most days when I am at Starbucks I lack the vocabulary, expression, and habits to notice God's glory in the present. I, like the people of Israel, desire a Moses to go up the mountain and deal with God for me. So I enlist the help of spiritual directors, pastors, holy women and men, teachers, gurus, books, devotionals, and retreats to do this work for me. I recently returned from a summer Christian camp where I served as a counselor for high school students. Many of them expressed in our small groups that this camp is the only place they feel close to God throughout their entire year. What a tragedy, considering that God's glory and presence is as much a part of their visit to the coffee shop with friends, as it is two hours away from home in the mountains. Silence, solitude, quiet times, and other spiritual disciplines are important, but rarely do the Scriptures actually prescribe in any certain terms these disciplines. But over and over *gratitude* is. We can learn much about how to listen to God (*humility*, explored in the previous chapter) and how to keep our life free of "static" (*simplicity*, which we explore in the next chapter) through spiritual practices and disciplines. But that life will be empty and disconnected if we are not grounded in the present and attentive to an experience of God today through what Paul says as "doing all in the name of the Lord Jesus, giving thanks to God the Father through him."[6]

6. Colossians 3:17 NIV

DO: WHAT SHOULD WE TRY TO DO? | GRATITUDE PRACTICES

I started my master's degree program while living in San Diego, CA. The closest satellite campus of Fuller Theological Seminary was in Irvine, right in the heart of Orange County. The commute was over seventy miles each way. During those long commutes I tried many different ways to pass the time: podcasts, audiobooks (some of my textbooks were on Audible), phone calls to family and friends, and prayer. One of the courses I took before moving north to Glendale (thus ending the necessity for the long commute), had a daunting assignment. We had to write down 100 things we were thankful for and praise God for each one. So using hands free, Siri on my iPhone, I created a note and kept adding the things I was praising God for. Of all the drives, this was the one I was most aware of the things around me and my own feelings and emotions. I had a sense of grounded-ness in the present experience because after the first ten or so I really had to work hard to come up with more. We are so used to thanking God for food, family, life, and the weather. Or in church singing praises about God's love, power, and creation but try to be specific 100 times!

Let *gratitude* be the gateway to other forms of virtue and character development in your life. Research has shown people who keep a journal of what they are thankful for results in higher satisfaction and meaning in life.[7] In Christian homes all around the world, the practice of prayer before meals is pretty standard. Some call it grace or a blessing for the food. Many times we ask God to help the food sustain and nourish our bodies—but Jesus' example is to give thanks. "When he had given thanks, he broke it and gave it to them saying, 'this is my body. . .'"[8] The examples are numerous. Feeding the five thousand. Appearing to the two disciples in Emmaus. In John's gospel when Jesus appears to the disciples gathered in a locked room. Each time it does not say he prayed or blessed the food but rather "gave thanks."[9] I want to urge you to see the

7. Emmons. *A handbook of models and measures.* 317–332

8. Matthew 26:26; Mark 14:22; Luke 22:19; 1 Corinthians 11:24 NIV

9. Matthew 14:19, 15:36, 26:26–27; Mark 6:41, 8:6–7, 14:22–23; Luke 9:16,

practices here as opportunities to give thanks to God, not some ritual or strategy for successful living but opportunities to pause and be grounded in the presence of God with you.

Journaling

Journaling can be a daily, weekly, or occasional practice. I want to stress the why and not the how here. I have found journaling to be something I find meaningful during certain seasons but not something I find enjoyable or life giving when I box myself into a required daily practice. The burden offsets and diminishes the joy. The why behind journaling has three compelling reasons. First, writing (and I prefer to use pen and paper) fleshes out what is in our minds into mature and complete thoughts. There are times to utter our thanks to God in silence and without words, to let our emotions fly with *gratitude*, but we are also reasoning creatures given the gift of logic and language. Using our words and capturing the complexities and intricacies is a beautiful thing. Journaling can take on the form of poetry and lyrics as well as a conversation. Second, writing allows us to revisit our moments of grounded-ness when we are adrift. Re-reading or simply skimming back through a *gratitude* journal can remind us of all we have to be thankful for. We can be our own best teacher. Third and finally, writing requires us to slowdown and stop multitasking. While I admire those great Christians like Brother Lawrence, who wrote the spiritual classic *The Practice of the Presence of God*, said he could pray just as well when washing the dishes or cleaning up as when in worship and solitude, my own experience is that the tasks I am doing dominate my mind. So writing, using our body to move our hand which moves the pen to write what our mind tells it, means we are fully engaged in the task with our whole self. Brevity is not a bad thing, in fact I would urge you to be more frequent and less lengthy rather than infrequent and long winded.

22:17, 19, 24:30; John 6:11 NIV

Gratitude Jar

Similar to journaling, the *gratitude* jar allows you to write out and collect moments and memories of what you are thankful for. In our home we call this a "Joy Jar", but regardless of what you call the jar, the practice is fairly simple. We use pieces of colored paper cut in small squares or strips to write down moments and things that have caused us joy for which we are grateful. At the end of the year we open the jar and take turns reading and remembering together. During special occasions like the holiday *Thanksgiving* we invite friends and family to add their joys and thanks to our jar as well.

Prayer of Examen

The Examen is a method of reviewing your day (the last twenty-four hours, week, month, or year) in the presence of God.[10] It's actually an attitude more than a method, a time set aside for thankful reflection on where God is in your everyday life. It has five steps, which most people take more or less in order, and it usually takes fifteen to twenty minutes to practice.

1. Become aware of God's presence.

Look back on the events of the day in the company of the Holy Spirit. The day may seem confusing to you—a blur, a jumble, a muddle. Ask God to bring clarity and understanding.

2. Give thanks.

Gratitude is the foundation of our relationship with God. Walk through your day in the presence of God and note its joys and delights. Focus on the day's gifts. Look at the work you did, the people you interacted with. What did you receive from these people? What did you give them? Pay attention to small things—the food you ate,

10. Adapted from Ignatian Spirituality, "The Daily Examen," n.d, https://www.ignatianspirituality.com/ignatian-prayer/the-examen/.

the sights you saw, and other seemingly small pleasures. God is in the details.

3. Review the day.

Talk with God about your day. Reflect on the feelings you experienced during the day. Boredom? Excitement? Resentment? Compassion? Anger? Confidence? What is God saying through these feelings? Notice your positive feelings. Anything negative? Bring before the Lord.

4. Express your feelings.

Ask the Holy Spirit to direct you to something during the day that God thinks is particularly important. It may involve a feeling—positive or negative. It may be a significant encounter with another person. Or it may be something that seems rather insignificant. Look at it. Pray about it. Allow the prayer to come right from your heart—whether a request, praise, repentance, or *gratitude*.

5. Look forward to tomorrow in hope.

What excites you about tomorrow? What do you want to hold onto from today that you make part of tomorrow? What do you want to let go of? Pay attention to the feelings that surface as you survey what's coming up. Are you doubtful? Cheerful? Apprehensive? Full of delighted anticipation? Allow these feelings to turn into prayer. Seek God's guidance. Ask him for help and understanding. Pray for hope.

Eucharist

One aspect of my church tradition for which I am truly thankful is the emphasis on having Communion, or the Lord's Supper, each week. My family cherished the practice so much that when we were members of a church that only shared communion monthly we would actually have a small "family worship" service on Sunday evenings to share in Communion. My first taste of wine was when we were traveling and could not find grape juice, so instead my mother diluted wine she found in the hotel mini bar with water. Remembering Jesus' body and blood was given by Jesus at Passover, a time when the people of Israel remembered their deliverance from Egypt with a special meal. In many church traditions, the Latin term Eucharist is still used to refer to the sharing of the two emblems of bread and juice. The word actually means "thanksgiving" and rightly so; we are giving thanks for Jesus' life, death, burial, and resurrection. You may be at a church like the ones I grew up at, where Communion was served every Sunday but it often lacked significance—what might it look like for you to cherish it? To bring significance to Communion no matter how your church practices it corporately. A mentor of mine shared a practice he and his wife have used and it has been extremely beneficial for my wife and I as well. (For any of my Presbyterian or more liturgical friends this will probably sound familiar). When the bread is passed, whoever is first to receive the plate says while serving the other "the body of Christ given for you" and likewise with the cup, when passed whoever receives it first says "the blood of Christ given for you." The other person after receiving the first blessing responds with "and also for you" after which we take the emblem at the same time together. I am intentional about sitting close to Janel when Communion is taking place, we have added to our practice holding hands while the prayer for the emblems is being offered. When we travel, if for some reason we are missing church that week or at a church that does not take communion on that Sunday we seek out emblems or plan ahead and pack our own. While there is nothing magical about the unleavened bread or the juice from grapes, I do believe there is something supernatural about remembering Jesus who died, was buried, and on the third day rose again. I believe when we center our lives and our *gratitude* on Jesus it does open up new paths of living into the virtues of Christ's character.

Chapter 4

Simplicity: The Way of Seeing

NOW: WHAT IS HAPPENING NOW? | BLINDNESS

Visualize the little old man from the Disney movie UP, sitting on a bar stool at the pulpit. We celebrated the 4th of July at my in laws in south Orange County and were at their church for worship and the retired pastor was sharing the communion meditation. This guy reminds me so much of my grandpa, a preacher from an era gone by. Full of so much wisdom and genuineness, a man you can trust. My wife leaned over to remind me that he is pretty much blind, but he still looks out boldly on those gathered. Before he began talking about communion he took a sidebar to share a little about the 4th of July. He said, "fireworks, that reminds me, have you heard about the girl who swallowed the firecrackers? Her hair came out in bangs!" I remember having a good laugh about that one, in fact I included it in the sermon I preached the next week. More memorable than the laughs and jokes, this older pastor had passion for God, for God's Word and for God's people. I have listened to this man's sermons and admired his ability to bring the Word alive through the scriptures— even without the ability to see his Bible! He is a powerful symbol for me of what I hope to embody as someone who proclaims Jesus and teaches others God's Word. Though he cannot see me sitting out in the pews and needs help walking up and down the stairs on the stage, he connects with me. He connects through laughter and deep insights on life, through firm confidence and empathizing pauses. Connection is so rare that when we find it we want to hold on to it for as long as we can. For this pastor, though his physical eyes have failed, God has gifted him with a unique way of connecting with others for many decades and still continues to do so.

In Scripture, physical blindness is often the visual used to describe the ignorance of humans to what God is up to. Jesus heals the sick and restores the sight of the blind. In fact this is at the center of Jesus' purpose in coming to Earth in human form. Luke captures Jesus' teaching on Isaiah in Luke chapter 4:

> [16] Jesus went to Nazareth, where he had been raised. On the Sabbath he went to the synagogue as he normally did and stood up to read. [17] The synagogue assistant gave him the scroll from the prophet Isaiah. He unrolled the scroll and found the place where it was written:
> [18] The Spirit of the Lord is upon me,
> because the Lord has anointed me.
> He has sent me to preach good news to the poor,
> to proclaim release to the prisoners
> and recovery of sight to the blind,
> to liberate the oppressed,
> [19] and to proclaim the year of the Lord's favor.
> [20] He rolled up the scroll, gave it back to the synagogue assistant, and sat down. Every eye in the synagogue was fixed on him. [21] He began to explain to them, "Today, this scripture has been fulfilled just as you heard it."[1]

Recovery of sight for the blind is part of the primary action and agency of Jesus in the world. The phrase "seeing is believing" is a message woven throughout our scientific method and rational reasoning culture. We have been raised in a culture of TV and events that claim you don't have to believe—because you can see for yourself. The invention of aircraft was a step from legend to reality. Now

---

1. Luke 4:16–21 CEB

no one scoffs at the idea of flying from LA to DC or around the world in a heavy metal cylinder. We run experiments to see the effects of something in order to prove it exists. For instance the classic gravity test is to take an object and drop it off a building. When I was in elementary school Bill Nye the Science Guy was on TV and I remember watching him drop a watermelon off a building to show the effects of gravity pulling the watermelon toward the ground. Seeing is an integral part of believing. Our eyes capture details even the best 4k camera cannot. Have you ever put on virtual reality goggles? Or rode in a simulator? Or gone to an IMAX movie? Often when you recall the experiences you describe them as life like, so real, 4D, or "I felt like I could reach out and touch it." Jesus comes in the power of the Holy Spirit to make God known. To make visible the invisible. To restore sight to our blindness caused by the separation we name as sin.

Sin is so much more than wrong stuff you do, secrets you keep, or pleasures God locks away like a parent locks away half the halloween candy of a four year old. Sin is missing out on connection with God. Yes, it does involve your actions. Stealing and lying disconnect us from others, especially from God. Yes, it does mean some things that seem sweet in the wrong quantity can cause aches or even catastrophic failure to vital organs. I have a type one diabetic cousin, but you would never know about it because of the medicines that saved, and continue to save, her life. Type two diabetes is the more familiar one, something drug companies often advertise treatments for on TV. The difference is that my cousin's pancreas had a catastrophic failure when she was two years old. The pancreas is what monitors the blood sugar levels in your body and any failure can lead to serious problems. Type two diabetes typically happens to people later in life and a common cause is obesity.

For type two diabetics, diet and exercise are better than most drugs and treatments. With type two diabetes, the body is creating too much sugar and it affects the body negatively as a whole. Once their pancreas can't keep up with the need for insulin, the body begins to shut down and blood sugar levels drop. The body needs a healthy pancreas in order to survive on it's own and function properly. Sin works in much the same fashion, slowly damaging or shutting down at times your spiritual and physical organs. There are shots available that can counteract the effects, but many of them are temporary fixes. Maybe you have advanced and gotten very good at compartmentalizing your life, but no matter how hard you work the damage is already done.

We should celebrate "fixes" to our emotional and spiritual needs just like we celebrate insulin shots or diet programs, but any personal trainer would tell you that a short term fix is a poor substitute to a healthy rhythm of good habits. A six month diet might help you lose a few pounds before your friend's wedding, but after that wedding you will likely gain more weight by returning to your old habits. What we are in need of is a lifestyle shift. I believe this is what Jesus wants us to see. To move beyond what Dallas Willard calls the "gospel of sin management" and into intimate relationship with God. To know God is the cure but it is not a quick, easy fix it requires a new way of seeing the world. *Simplicity.*

Caught up with all the frantic activity of every day's demands, we are full of noise. I love how the Apostle Paul describes life, "we see as through a glass darkly."[2] The picture is hazy and fuzzy like an old TV set trying to get a signal. And just like your grandpa who was tired and angry with the static, sometimes the only thing we respond to is a great big fist to the top of our control box. But hitting rock bottom or smashing headlong into trouble is not the only thing that brings clarity. *Simplicity* is the opportunity to remove the clutter and see more clearly the truth of what is. We could go on with all the static and noise but that would mean we are simply living through all the mess. What if instead we chose a different way of seeing our world and circumstances? What if we saw God a different way? What if we lived simply? I believe *simplicity* is a spiritual way of seeing. With eyes wide open we can be thankful to God and the clarity allows us to lean in by listening humbly to God and others. Without *simplicity* we stampede our way through life with blinders on, ignorant to God's presence and love in our lives.

2. 1 Corinthians 13:12 KJV

KNOW: WHAT DO WE KNOW ABOUT GOD? | PEACE AND PREPARATION

I was with my family at Papa's Pizza, a local pizza parlor in Eugene, celebrating my dad's birthday. My grandpa was there, who we call "Papa". I was chatting with Papa, at Papa's pizza. He said "Lars, I have your next text for a sermon or devotional." Growing up, some of my favorite conversations with Papa revolved around the Bible. Still today, I value his input on sermons and his thoughts on unique passages. "I don't remember where it is found, but I was reading the Psalms the other day and came across a verse that said 'righteousness has kissed peace'" he said. Well isn't that quite the imagery, and from Papa no less! Needless to say I was real curious. When I got in the car I promptly looked up "righteousness kissed peace" in my Bible app. Sure enough, Psalm 85.

> [1] You, Lord, showed favor to your land; you restored the fortunes of Jacob. [2] You forgave the iniquity of your people and covered all their sins. [3] You set aside all your wrath and turned from your fierce anger. [4] Restore us again, God our Savior, and put away your displeasure toward us. [5] Will you be angry with us forever? Will you prolong your anger through all generations? [6] Will you not revive us again, that your people may rejoice in you? [7] Show us your unfailing love, Lord, and grant us your salvation. [8] I will listen to what God the Lord says; he promises peace to his people, his faithful servants—but let them not turn to folly. [9] Surely his salvation is near those who fear him, that his glory may dwell in our land. [10] Love and faithfulness meet together; righteousness and peace kiss each other.[3]

I don't know about you, but the first I time I read this passage the first part really bogged me down. What is this all talking about? I know the Psalms are poetry, and the authors (these guys in particular are called the Sons Of Korah) were often singers—but I am really not sure what all of this means. So I thought, thanks Papa,

---

3. Psalm 85:1–10 NIV

closed my iPad, and mostly forgot about the Psalm and all the questions it raised.

A month later, my brother and I were at the movies with a friend from church and her parents. We sat down in our seats, about midway from the screen. I put the popcorn on the floor and prepared to kick back with my feet up on the seats in front of me. I stopped, however, because I happened to be sitting next to our friends mother. She was younger than my parents were but I got to thinking she might think like my mom does, "don't put your dirty shoes on the back of the chairs." This is not usually a problem because my mom likes to sit in the middle of the row that has the railing in front. She does not mind us putting our feet up on the railing, in fact some times she indulges with us. The previews were starting, I had spent a considerable amount of time on the internal evaluation of the appropriate placement of my feet. I reached down to indulge in the popcorn. As I did, I noticed the silhouette of someone in the seat in front of me. How embarrassing would it have been if, with my dirty shoes on, I had kicked forward this guys seat. Now I was befuddled. How had I, a pretty observant person, missed seeing him? A closer look was needed. As I repositioned myself to observe the seat in front of me I realized why I had missed him. He and his girlfriend were slumped down in their seats making out. I do not want to gross you out, but let's say they were taking advantage of the low lights. The intimacy I witnessed between them was more than I wanted to see. A quick peck is all fair game, but a whole preview plus length kiss—come on now! Just before the movie began I was tempted to kick their chair and let them know they were not being as subtle as they thought. But just then the previews ended and the couple retreated back to their respective seats.

On the way out of the movie theater I could not help but bring up what had transpired. Others had also noticed something conspicuous about the couple and added to the story. We kept bringing up the fact it was just too intimate for a public place. The parents took the opportunity to do some instruction for their daughter and the two impressionable young men they had in tow. When I got home and found myself telling the story to my parents it just seemed comical. Who would want the world to see that level of intimacy? Who wants everyone else to be in on your love and how you are getting to know each other that way? There are some things that should not be done in public venues.

PDA, public displays of affection, are actually a huge deal. In youth ministry, we have inherited some less than helpful camp slogans like: "no purple" (boys are blue and girls are pink, so if you mix them you get purple). Or "leave room for Jesus." My favorite dumb tradition was a camp midnight hike on which guys and girls could ask each other on a "date" but they could not hold hands, so they would get a short stick and each hold the stick. All of these PDA rules were meant to restrict students from ever getting too intimate. Having been married for almost five years now, I realize the opposite is also true. There are PDA rules your spouse has never told you but they want you to observe them. Things like holding their hand in public, stroking their back, looking them in the eye across the room. . .etc. Some of the best marriage advice around sexual intimacy was given to me by my dad. He encouraged me to notice the hinderances like a messy room, dirty dishes in the kitchen, or the words of encouragement in the morning. Night time intimacy actually starts in the morning and continues throughout the day and is often linked to the small public intimate moments shared.

Our tendency is to view public displays of affection like the intense kissing of the movie theater couple as too much. I describe it like how I watch any movie that has intense parts in it: finger spread in front of face. I am watching it happen, but my reaction is "ahh too much, I should not be seeing this, I do not want to see this"; yet at the same time I am attracted to seeing it. I cannot look away. Could this be what the authors of Psalm 85 are getting at? As I was telling the story and fanned the fingers in front of my face and said jokingly "too much kissing" I remembered what Papa had told me about Psalm 85, "there is an intimate relationship between righteousness and peace."

Let that sink in for a moment, "there is an intimate relationship between righteousness and peace." What does that evoke in you? How do you react to righteousness most often? Why does peace kiss righteousness, why not success or purpose? The whole text is centered on this understanding of righteousness. In fact when you read the verses that follow it becomes even more pointed:

> Love and faithfulness meet together; righteousness and peace kiss each other. Faithfulness springs forth from the earth, and righteousness looks down from heaven. The Lord will indeed give what is good, and our land will yield its harvest. Righteousness goes before him and prepares the way for his steps.[4]

The word pictures in the Psalms are just beautiful. The Sons of Korah weave a masterful painting. Righteousness is said to be looking down out of the majestic clouds with rays of light onto a golden harvest field. The Willamette valley in Oregon, where I grew up, is amazing and the seasons bring tremendous beauty. Living now in Los Angeles I miss those seasons. I remember visiting my grandmother's farm. She had several cows that she would feed with the hay harvested from the fifteen acres of property. If the grass was as tall as I was, haying time was just around the corner. The summer months in Oregon can get up to around 100 degrees which is essential for a good hay harvest. Once you cut the hay, you use a special rake to turn the hay and make rows. Then a bailer, typically towed behind a tractor, creates the desired size of bales. Once it's dry from the heat, you can use it as feed for your animals. Once the grass turns to a bright golden brown from it's original green color, you know it's ready. There was tremendous preparation that took place for the harvest to come in. My job was to salt the hay bales as they were being loaded in the barn (until I got big enough to hoist the bales onto the trailer or stack inside the barn). Salt takes the moisture away. Just like the sun drying out the cut hay before we could bale it, the salt was there to prevent the hay from getting moist in the barn. This is a tall order if you know anything about Oregon weather. The rain could come anytime and throughout the year people work to fight against mold and mildew from the constant wet, moist air. What is so wrong with hay being moist? For one it can be unhealthy and no longer fit to feed the cows, but much worse is when the moisture and mildew develop they can spontaneously

4. Psalm 85:10–13 NIV

combust! The erosion process can actually cause fires and burn whole barns down in the dead of winter!

Salt was part of the preparation process for bringing in the harvest. Peace is like the harvest. Peace is beautiful but it takes some time and preparation to grow into the golden harvest. Peace requires salt and stacking to reap the actual bounty of peace. Righteousness, says the psalmist, is that preparation. So what is righteousness? One of those religious terms that gets used in songs, repeated in prayers, preached from the pulpit, and generally ignored in daily life. We might find ourselves saying it when we quote Crush, the Australian sea turtle, from the movie *Finding Nemo*, "Righteous, righteous!" In which instance we can deduce the meaning is akin to awesome or right on, words and phrases used to describe something that is done well. This slang usage of righteous can actually help us reclaim the meaning of this religious word. "Righteousness is fulfillment of the expectations in any relationship, whether with God or other people."[5] For something to be righteous means that the relationship is done well.

I attended a funeral service for the grandmother of a couple of my youth group students. I was reminded of the beauty from relationships done well in the stories everyone shared and the memories they wanted to impart to us. Funerals and memorials are some of the few places we still pay attention to righteousness. The poorer qualities of a persons life are often left outside the doors. The pictures chosen highlight the prime of life and how we want our loved one to be remembered. I can recall at many a memorial service someone sharing this remark "I know when they got to the gates they heard 'well done, my good and faithful servant.'"[6] We all desire that message to be spoken of us, that we would have lived a life worthy of "well done." This is what righteousness means. To be able to say that our relationship with God is done well, that we fulfilled the expectations. But this is just not the focus of our busy days. Everyone wants peace, they want the result of righteousness but not the hard work of forming the daily habits of living done well.

5. Elwell. *Baker Encyclopedia of the Bible.* 1860
6. Matthew 25:21 NIV

What about the word peace? The word in the original language is Shalom and carries great depth. The Hebrew greeting for which our english equivalent is peace means a state of well being. This can account for our common usage of peace being the absence of war or conflict. For instance when I visit family gatherings, a win is for the house to be peaceful. So when I walk in there are times I want to literally greet them with peace, because I know it will be a richer time if there is an absence of conflict. But just avoiding conflict does not actually enter me into a state of shalom. The psalmist was envisioning a state of well being that exists even amid the conflict and devastation of war, violence, and suffering. With these definitions, a paraphrase of the passage "righteousness and peace kiss each other" could be: relationship done well and a state of well being are intimately connected.

Simplicity is the preparation, the righteousness that our lives need. The challenge is how quickly practices that are meant to remove the static can become "self-righteous" one ups. Or we join cliques that create their own set of religious laws calling them "righteous" ways of removing the fog from hearing God but they themselves become the distraction. *Simplicity* is about preparation but discretion is advised.

> [16] [Then Jesus] told them a story: "A rich man had a fertile farm that produced fine crops. [17] He said to himself, 'What should I do? I don't have room for all my crops.' [18] Then he said, 'I know! I'll tear down my barns and build bigger ones. Then I'll have room enough to store all my wheat and other goods. [19] And I'll sit back and say to myself, "My friend, you have enough stored away for years to come. Now take it easy! Eat, drink, and be merry!"' [20] "But God said to him, 'You fool! You will die this very night. Then who will get everything you worked for?' [21] "Yes, a person is a fool to store up earthly wealth but not have a rich relationship with God."
>
> [22] Then, turning to his disciples, Jesus said, "That is why I tell you not to worry about everyday life—whether you have enough food to eat or enough clothes to wear. [23] For life is more than food, and your body more than clothing. [24] Look at the ravens. They don't plant or harvest

or store food in barns, for God feeds them. And you are far more valuable to him than any birds! [25] Can all your worries add a single moment to your life? [26] And if worry can't accomplish a little thing like that, what's the use of worrying over bigger things?. . .[29] "And don't be concerned about what to eat and what to drink. Don't worry about such things. [30] These things dominate the thoughts of unbelievers all over the world, but your Father already knows your needs. [31] Seek the Kingdom of God above all else, and he will give you everything you need.

[32] "So don't be afraid, little flock. For it gives your Father great happiness to give you the Kingdom. [33] "Sell your possessions and give to those in need. This will store up treasure for you in heaven! And the purses of heaven never get old or develop holes. Your treasure will be safe; no thief can steal it and no moth can destroy it. [34] Wherever your treasure is, there the desires of your heart will also be.[7]

Hitting a bit close to home? Or maybe you just glossed over it again, having heard this passage preached or taught in Bible study. Perhaps we hear this passage in "bible speak" not challenging or convicting because the words or metaphors are not as relevant to a 21st century life. I do not consider myself a "rich man" but considering I live in Southern California and live comfortably means I am rich compared to the majority of the world's population. I do not think Jesus is speaking only to the millionaire here, but those with plenty. We too often subscribe to a message that there is not enough and so we pursue excess. Not one car but two. Not one bedroom but four. Not one plate but as many as you want. The rich man is not condemned for having plenty or being wealthy, the problem actually became his infatuation and obsession with the stuff. He received a blessing, a gift, an overflowing abundance but instead of enjoying it and being generous he wanted to anticipate more and hoard what he had. His excuse for the obsession was planning for the future. This does make logical sense; what if there were a famine, stock market crash, economic downturn, or disease that wiped out a season of crops? Isn't it smart to save up and plan ahead? I

7. Luke 12:16–34 NIV

am not saying you shouldn't contribute to an IRA or retirement plan, but when saving becomes an obsession and steals your joy then even a good idea has become your idol and has replaced God. This is where Jesus is going.

Stuff or treasure, as Jesus calls it, is a great litmus test of the heart. Jesus' story of the guy who is introduced as a wise, smart, logical, business man who makes it big and is successful ends by calling him a fool who dies without being in a "rich relationship" with God. After this story are a set of maxims or proverbs. These teachings unravel the most basic ideas about life as humans: food, clothing, worry. Can you set the book down for a minute and do something for me? Open your notes app on your phone or grab a sheet of paper (maybe use the margin of the page right here) and try to name what you had for dinner last week. Food is pretty essential, and as a parent I am more aware now that I need to make sure and plan meal times. As I am writing this our daughter is still eating blended food and primarily breastfeeding. So if I as the dad am in charge for the day I better have some milk along with me and some special solids that are mom approved. Ashlynn is dependent upon me to feed her and to care for her properly. She is not old enough or developed enough to request food or to worry about where her next meal is coming from. She trusts that Janel and I will provide it for her. I know Jesus is not advocating we neglect common sense and wait around for bread to fall from the sky—rather I believe Jesus is challenging our obsession. What if instead of building bigger barns to contain our obsessions we were content with what we had. We celebrated in the times of excess and trusted in the times of want. I have adapted part of the Lord's prayer that goes "give us our daily bread" to a phrase "help me discern between the things that I need and the things I want." What if before the new iPhone came out we prayed that simple phrase? What if before we run headlong into grasping for more we paused to take inventory of what we already have? Before we go Black Friday shopping again or create another Christmas wish list, what if we made a trust list? I think Jesus is using the very basics of human existence to challenge us. The people he likely was speaking to did not live like the rich man with excess. They probably experienced hunger and may have lived pay check to pay check. To have excess, so much that one would need to build a bigger barn, was what most of them dreamed and longed for. Much like my desire to build a bigger, cooler, grander house every time I watch "Love it or List it" on HGTV. Jesus came to announce how that will only blind them and distract them from life with God. In fact, the way to become rich in heavenly standards is to give away and sell.

Jesus closes this teaching section with an invitation to "seek first the kingdom of God" which is the purpose of the discipline and practice of *Simplicity*. This means we may have to rid ourselves not just of the desires for more but actually take action with the possessions and stuff we already have. Jesus knows this will make us afraid, there is risk in this counter logic move of giving up. And there lies the turn. Unlike food, clothing, and stuff in our lives we do not purchase the presence of God in our lives. There is not a limited quantity of the "Kingdom" out there that has to be bought up before it is gone. This is why the barn story is so critical. Food, shelter, clothing, protection, success, plenty—these are all blessings from God but they are not God. They come from God but when we make them the focus of our attention and obsess over them we actually become miserable because we miss out on God. When stuff is not our focus, when we actually give up and sell then our hearts become freed and unfettered to the stuff. This is the beauty of *simplicity*—the heart that is no longer a slave to possessions is free to know God. There is nothing wrong with finding joy in a new Nintendo game, like Super Smash Brothers Ultimate on the Switch, but if I was obsessed with it and guarded it I would miss out on the even greater joy of seeing my nieces and nephews play Mario Kart for the first time. Even though the three year old throws the remote on the ground, I can relax because it is simply stuff. This passage has so convicted me regarding my Amazon Prime shopping that I physically blocked Amazon from my phone for three months. The practice of having to actually go to a physical store to buy something caused me to have moments where I stopped and asked the question: what if instead of buying this I gave something away?

DO: WHAT SHOULD WE TRY TO DO? | SIMPLICITY PRACTICES

Abraham Maslow created a hierarchy of needs. If you have traveled outside your own bubble you will notice that not everyone has the same needs being met. The home in Vietnam my family lived in was on a dirt road that had a high wall, gate, swimming pool, and a guard shack with someone there 24/7. Just across the street lived a local Vietnamese family in a make shift home with metal roofing all around. I had needs, but my needs were drastically different from the needs of the children who played on the street, or the garbage man who was accosted by our blue tick coon hound every week. Maslow discovered that as people's basic needs are met (food, shelter, safety) their quality of life began to be determined by psychological needs (belonging and self esteem). The top of the pyramid is self-fulfillment or self actualization. These, you might say, are the individuals who we might catagorize from afar as people who "have it all" or are "living the dream." We want to move into being who we truly are meant to be, to achieve our biggest dreams, and tap into our full potential but we lack the capacity to do so because we are still dealing with our unmet psychological needs.[8]

8. Saul McLeod, "Maslow's Hierarchy of Needs," Simply Psychology, May 21, 2018, https://www.simplypsychology.org/maslow.html.

So where are you on the hierarchy of needs? Are you like my neighbors in Vietnam grasping for basic needs? If so it may be much harder to address psychological needs or not on your radar to address the self-fulfillment ones. Or perhaps you are more like I was, having all my basic needs met but still very needy when it came to psychological needs. Out of our neediness we demand things of those around us. Brené Brown has spent over a decade doing research with regard to shame. She says in her book *The Gifts of Imperfection* "we can only love others as much as we love ourselves."[9] You will end up projecting your shame and neediness onto those around you—a frightening prospect when our aim is righteous (done well) relationships. Today, the present, reality, current state, this season, where you are now—these are all names for what is happening in your life. Before we can grow we have to know where we are. Coaches and fitness trainers always do a "fitness test" at the start of training so they and their athlete know how to measure improvement. Without the "fitness test" it is hard to recognize growth and make appropriate goals and fitness plan. Ask yourself these questions:

- Physically: How would you rate your overall physical health (your mind and body)? What one or two habits/practices are currently going well / life giving? Is there a negative habit or practice you currently are doing / life draining?

- Spiritually: How would you rate your overall spiritual health (relationship with God)? What one or two habits/practices are currently going well / life giving? Is there a negative habit or practice you are currently doing / life draining?

- Relationally: How would you rate your overall relational health (relationships with other people)? What one or two habits/practices are currently going well / life giving? Is there a negative habit or practice you are currently doing / life draining?

Your shalom, state of well being, is not about how much money you are making or the prestige of your position or the number of children you have or the size of your Instagram following. Your

9. Brown. *The Gifts of Imperfection*. 26

state of well being is how well your needs are met. Unlike Maslow I see your hierarchy of needs being three fold: physical, spiritual, and relational. Much of the same dynamics captured in Maslow's pyramid fit within this three fold framework as well. A state of being physically unhealthy takes priority because your mind and body constitute your immediate reality. Every day you get up, walk around, breathe, and engage with others using your mind and body. Decisions and choices are set before us, whether to order a Love it or Gotta Have it at Cold Stone or perhaps more long term like who I should marry or what career path I should take. One particular shift I make personally is to move spiritual needs in before relational needs. This is intentional. I believe we are all spiritual, even if someone does not claim a particular faith or practice any adherence to a religious group. As people we worship and give our allegiance to things. James K. A. Smith recently published a book *You Are What You Love* where he makes the claim that shopping malls and stadiums have become the new religious shrines of our day. What we love is what we worship, this gets back to the Christian point of view about worship: loving God. We are seeking this deep intimacy with God, to know God as we are known. When this need goes unmet or met in an unhealthy way I believe relationships with other people are much more difficult. The third sphere of relational needs flows out of the first two. A healthy physical (mind and body) person who knows God can enter into knowing others beyond the simple niceties of "hi, how are you" to the depths of care and compassion. Relational needs most often center around being understood. We would do well to develop the capacity to listen well (*humility*) in order to develop empathy for the other person, which is truly what we desire for others to do for us. The way we treat those closest to us is an indicator for how we will treat everyone else. All of these, but especially the relational needs, flow out of our own self love. I think it's worth reminding you of that quote from Brené Brown again: "you cannot love someone more than you love yourself."[10]

10. Brown. *The Gifts of Imperfection.* 26

You should not be ashamed to consider your own state of well being. It is incredibly important for you to have a clear picture, but what you do with that picture is the work that requires real effort. People pay thousands of dollars to sit with gurus, life coaches, or therapists in order to have help in deciding what to do with their self understanding. Tony Robbins is a famous example of someone who helps people get real with where they are and create manageable changes to their habits to achieve their dreams. After watching his documentary on Netflix *Not Your Guru,* I was impressed by the need people have for straight, sometimes brutal, honesty. We can all cry along as we see the transformations happen on Netflix or tv but our own state of well being often escapes our grasp. I believe this is where the practices of *simplicity* come in.

Relationship done well and a state of well being are intimately connected. Jesus knew this to be true so he summed up all of Scripture with a single phrase: love God and love others. When our relationship with God is done well (righteousness) we can be in a state of well being with others (shalom). This is the key to the intimate relationship between righteousness and peace. Relationship done well with God brings heaven to earth and prepares the harvest of peace. This is why this book has centered on asking the question: what does relationship done well with God look like? I believe the journey is about following in the way of Jesus who modeled *humility, gratitude,* and *simplicity.* To do this we must imagine a new truly Crush like "Righteous, righteous" life that prepares the way for a "peace that passes all understanding," a life with less noise.[11]

In the following pages, I want to share three general principles regarding *simplicity* and then name a specific practice that corresponds with each principle that I have found helpful. I believe the principles are what will help you name different specific practices for the season of life you are in. Unlike the principles, these practices may need changing and tweaking as we grow and change. "The purpose of the Spiritual Disciplines," Richard Foster says, "is the total transformation of the person. . ." by ". . .replacing old destructive

---

11. Philippians 4:7 NIV

habits of thought with new life-giving habits."[12] I like to paraphrase him this way: Know what should be held tight (principles) and what you can hold loosely (specific practices). There will be times when a practice or habit no longer is life-giving and may need to be jettisoned or reworked in order to regain the intent behind the principle.

Solitude

The Principle: Being removed from external stimulation and distraction to know oneself and create space for communion with the God, the Holy One.

Solitude often has a companion: silence. These two things work well together to help remove distractions. Meditative practices can be helpful, but unlike many forms of meditation, the goal is not to empty ourselves completely or to find our inner peace, but rather to remove or empty the distractions making way for the Holy Spirit to fill us. The peace we experience is not made of our own making but is the peace of God which transcends all understanding. Practices could range from intentional moments of solitude to longer multi day retreats. The important thing is not finding the perfect practice but rather building some sort of solitude practice into our regular rhythms. As an extrovert, I find solitude and silence both incredibly difficult to cultivate. I want to fill my life with noise and people. Perhaps you are not like this and solitude comes more naturally. Still, you need to cultivate an intentional solitude practice; one that is not selfish or borne out of avoiding healthy interactions with others.

12. Foster. *Celebration of Discipline.* 62

A Practice: Centering Prayer.

Centering prayer, sometimes called contemplative prayer, involves setting aside a period of time to be in silence. This silent and wordless prayer time is about surrender and trusting God by letting go of thoughts which come to our mind. I recommend you get some instruction from a spiritual mentor or teacher on how to practice Centering Prayer. I begin my day in the morning with 15 minutes and have so many crazy thoughts that I spend most of my time acknowledging them and releasing them. The goal or object is not to be empty (like many forms of meditation) but to practice surrendering control of our lives to God. Trust requires that we simply let go and let God. This is much easier to say than do, so the daily Centering Prayer conditions me to be better. The spiritual teacher who taught me Centering Prayer, Joe Stabile, says, "When we practice Centering Prayer every day. . .it changes from being a place we go to and becomes where we come from."

Sabbath

The Principle: Breaking away from normal activity patterns for rest and play to appreciate the good work done and create space for the creative work ahead.

Sabbath is rooted in two aspects of Jewish history found in the Old Testament: creation and exodus. The normal pattern in Genesis 1 is creating until day seven when God breaks the pattern. Sabbath keeping is commanded to Israel in Deuteronomy 5's repeat of the 10 commandments with a different reason given: remember God rescued you from slavery. Sabbath is a break from the slavery of productivity and work. Today many are enslaved, whether by economic pressures (poverty or extremely high costs of living) or cultural pressures (like the American Dream) to work themselves to death. Sabbath keeping is a regular reminder that we too are God's creation. Finite bodies, with the need for rhythms. Sabbath breaks our normal patterns and reminds us we are not slaves but free. Practices may look like creating boundaries around our work/home life when we are unavailable to email or social media. Other practices may be building in hobbies which interrupt our normal patterns and rejuvenate us, allowing us for that period of time to let go of all the stresses of our lives and simply be with God. Some may consider weekly, monthly, and yearly ways to incorporate Sabbath practices. An important reminder is the communal nature of Sabbath keeping in Scripture. God rests and invites humanity into rest on the seventh day. As part of the 10 commandments, Sabbath keeping was a communal law code to shape how the whole community of Israel were to live together. As you discern practices, invite your loved ones to speak into them and how you will practice them. This could be a close friend, spouse, child, roommate, church group, etc. Try to allow the Sabbath to influence how you do life together.

A Practice: Techno Sabbath.

Our cell phones are with us all the time. We often wake up to them and send messages or scroll social media as the last thing we do before sleep. We pass the time with Spotify or watching Netflix. Our homes are filled with what Andy Crouch calls "glowing rectangles." Several times a year (usually three or four Saturdays) our family turns off the phones for eight hours and go do something outdoors. A beach trip, riding bikes, hiking, or making dinner and playing board games at home. For safety we usually put one phone in our backpack but we try to wakeup naturally without an alarm and simply let the day unfold. Obviously in this day and age, it's hard to totally avoid technology unless you go somewhere really remote. But these scheduled times of unplugging can help us retreat for a time from the frantic, fast pace of the world we live in of always being connected.

Stuff

The Principle: Identifying the usefulness and attachment to our possessions in order to understand where we have placed our heart and passion.

Stuff may not seem spiritual at all. In fact I am combining many spiritual disciplines under one roof and coining a new name: Stuff. Solitude is concerned with slowing down the speed of the interior life and Sabbath is concerned with slowing down the speed of the exterior life. Both are interrupters meant to be used to recenter ourselves. Stuff is where our interior life meets our exterior life. The things we possess demonstrate our priorities and the condition of our heart while also dominating our time and requiring our attention. Therefore being both good care takers of resources and unencumbered by clutter is food for the entire mind, body, and soul. The practices will range from the food we eat, tidiness around the house, budgets we follow, clothes we wear, to the purchases we make. Certainly more loose of a definition, but equally as important to the task of practicing *simplicity* and removing the static.

A Practice: 90 Day Amazon Fast.

It is often remarked that in 21 days you can make a new habit. But many researchers I have read challenge that by stating it is not until the 90 day marker that the habit becomes established. I chose to do a 90 day Amazon fast, meaning I had to go to a physical store to get the random stuff I wanted. This actually challenged me because I needed to put more thought into the items I was getting. Do I really need this? Amazon offers easy access and one day or next day shipping. All of the benefits are great but the fast helped me evaluate my spending habits.

To finish the chapter on *simplicity* I wanted to share the list of ten ideas, with my added reflections, from Richard Foster's *Celebration of Discipline*. This was the first book that captured my imagination about *simplicity* being a core virtue and spiritual practice.

Adapted from Richard Fosters 10 practices in *Celebration of Discipline*.[13]

1. **Buy things for their usefulness rather than their status.** Before buying ask three simple questions: 1) why am I buying this? 2) how will I use this "thing?" 3) what does this "thing" communicate about my priorities?

2. **Reject anything that is producing an addiction in you.** Addiction is serious. If you are struggling with a drug, alcohol, gambling, or other addiction please seek professional help or join a support group. For those of us who tend to use the word somewhat more flippantly like "I am so addicted to this new Netflix show" we may want to be more careful with the word. Still, Foster's point rings true. We ought to reject anything that we use repeatedly to cope but ends up producing a need within us to satisfy it over and over. TV, social media, email, food, recreational drugs, that drink to take the edge off, masturbation, hooking up, exercise, gaming, thrill seeking. . .

3. **Develop a habit of giving things away.** Have you ever watched a reality show about hoarders? You often see people that are living with only pathways to navigate through their piles of stuff. The host of the show stages an intervention to help the hoarder see just how untenable their life is with all this stuff. The person usually agrees and breaks down in tears thanking them for the help. But the next day when the dumpster arrives and sorting begins, they sing a different tune. You may not consider yourself a hoarder but we all have opportunities to asses how much stuff we have. With places like GoodWill and the Salvation Army, giving things away has become as easy as dropping it off. Janel and I have found it useful to adopt a "one for one" principle. Whenever we buy an article of clothing, we

13. Foster. *Celebration of Discipline*. 90–95

have to donate or throw away a like item from our existing col-
lection. We still have too many clothes but we are beginning to
see the joy it brings to give away and get rid of things. Rather
than feeling like we have to hold onto everything we have, we
are finding great freedom in regular habits of giving away and
reducing.

4. **Refuse to be propagandized by the custodians of modern
   gadgetry.** As I write this Apple and Disney have just released
   their streaming platforms to compete with Netflix and Amazon Prime. Every few months a new product or updated one
   is released from Google, Microsoft, Apple, and other tech
   companies with a promise to make our lives better and more
   enjoyable. Much of the marketing seems to be selling a product to fix a problem we did not even recognize before. In fact
   many of the gadgets require other gadgets in order to be efficient and useful (I'm thinking of smart home devices like
   a google home which requires you to buy smart compatible
   light bulbs or switches). We need to check our motives before
   subscribing to narrative given us by companies like Apple: is
   this really something I need? Is the problem they are offering
   this product as a solution to really a problem I have or need
   to be solved?

5. **Learn to enjoy things without owning them.** My parents pur-
   chased a used Lexus convertible to make driving to Southern
   California for visits more enjoyable. I distinctly remember
   listening to this section of Richard Foster's book on Audible
   while driving their Lexus around San Diego. They had come
   to visit on their way to a work trip of my dad's in Sri Lanka.
   So they drove down and flew out of LAX. I got to baby sit
   their car for six weeks—rough life I know. I rarely drove my
   own car during that time unless I needed more than two seats.
   There were many a night where I looked to see if I could afford
   getting my own convertible, but these words "enjoy things
   without owning them" reverberated through my mind. This is
   probably the most difficult habit for me to form.

6. **Develop a deeper appreciation for the creation.** Go outdoors. Perhaps like me you live in a city that feels like endless concrete and pavement, but there can still be moments and places that bring you in touch with God's creativity. The guava tree in our small yard is something I often catch myself staring at amidst the noise and chaos of the city. But even here I can find the reminder of God's creativity and goodness. Hiking and skiing in the mountains, swimming in the ocean, waking with the sunrise or watching the sunset, walking in a park, sitting by a stream, fishing on the lake or sailing on the ocean—these all have been intentional ways for me to see God's creative nature. All that is required is to simply take note of what is around you and available to you and go.

7. **Look with a healthy skepticism at all "buy now, pay later" schemes.** Lay away, credit cards, lines of credit, loans—theses are not evil. However, they can become burdensome and distracting. Debt of any kind is a burden and weight you carry. Not all credit, loans, or payment plans are bad ideas but just because you can do it does not necessarily mean it is wise to. The best way to avoid rash financial decisions is to run them by someone you trust with your honesty about finances. Have these conversations often. Talking openly and honestly about mistakes you've made and loans you currently have will help you to be wiser in the future. Avoiding these conversations and accountability partners will only lead you to repeat the mistakes because you will be burying the feelings of shame and hiding even from yourself.

8. **Obey Jesus' instructions about plain, honest speech.** Re-read Matthew 5:33–37 and James 5:12. These passages are worth pondering and discussing with others. They can help you to understand how to embrace clear, direct, and honest speech without the white lies and other forms of deception. We need to be consistent as well, not talking behind others backs, gossiping, or spinning up stories.

9. **Reject anything that breeds the oppression of others.** Fair trade products have gained popularity recently, which has

caused many people to take a more critical look at the practices of multinational corporations dealing in things like diamonds, coffee, cocoa, clothing, manufacturing, and others. In college, Janel and I had the privilege to go on a mission trip to Cambodia and work with an organization combating sex trafficking and other forms of child slavery. In places of poverty there is great risk for human trafficking, but the dark reality is just how much of it goes on all around the world including in developed countries like the U.S.A. Not all of us will be able to afford the time to research every item of clothing or product we purchase, but we can become more aware and act on that awareness. This means being conscious that our activism is not simply pushing "like" or "love" on a Facebook campaign to end human trafficking but extends even into the companies and organizations we support with our ongoing business. Climate change, renewable energy, water, trash, recycling, thrifting, and so much more are opportunities to engage beyond traditional boycotts of large multinational companies.

10. **Shun anything that distracts you from seeking first the kingdom of God.** I like to think of this as Foster's catch all. Schedule a meeting with your pastor or spiritual director; someone who can help you discern and flesh out practically what the kingdom of God looks like. I often define the kingdom of God as the "presence" of God in my life. This may mean you need to let go of that Netflix show you are binging because it becomes all that you think about or want to do when you are at home. Perhaps this distracts you from being aware of and seeking the presence of God. Hobbies, activities, busyness, work, and relationships are all good things in moderation. With the help of someone wise in your life, you may need to assess what things need to be "shunned" because they're keeping you from seeking a deeper awareness of God with you.

Learning Prayer

Humility moves us to see prayer as listening to God rather than always talking. *Gratitude* changes our prayer from requests regarding the future to helping us be grounded in the present by acknowledging our thanks for what God has done and is doing in our lives. The new instruction on prayer which *Simplicity* gives is to move from a set point and time into a practice of the always and ever presence of God with us. *Simplicity* allows us to press into the reality of Paul's exhortation to "pray without ceasing" like we see in the life of Christians like Brother Lawrence in *The Practice of the Presence of God*. James the brother of Jesus puts it this way, "come close to God [with a contrite heart] and He will come close to you."[14] The message Jesus is trying to send us often gets lost in the static of life—much like the static our radios, TVs, WiFi signals, and cell signal often receive. *Simplicity* is not the end game, rather it is the practice of dialing in the frequency in order to pay attention to God's presence already among us.

14. James 4:8 AMP

Chapter 5

Rhythms: Habits for Knowing God

NOW: WHAT IS HAPPENING NOW? | GRAPES AND ROUTINES

One day when we were younger, I was playing outside with my brother and the two other youngest cousins in the family. The overgrowth was a fantastic wonderland for five year olds to play in. We found grapes buried under some berry vines and overgrown grass. After eating the grapes we could find, my brother ran over to the electric cow fence and stuck his hands right on it. Ouch! The other three of us ran over to check that he was still alive and breathed a sigh of relief when we realized we wouldn't have to tell my mom we killed him! Sometimes the journey of finding the fruit we are after can be a shocking one. Our lives are so overgrown and tangled with thorns that we do not see the caution signs saying "do not touch." The obvious one would be binge watching Netflix or TV, constant scrolling in your favorite social media app, or the comparison game found in fashion magazines and Facebook pages. We realize that all of these have good fruit of entertainment or connection but they also come with a nasty bite if we ignore the warning signs—and they can even bring about deadly things like depression.

Fast forward two decades to the same farm but now the overgrown grapes have been tended. New vines have been planted in other locations. One set of vines have been trained up an arbor. Now even more beautiful clusters of grapes droop overhead as my brother sits with his beautiful bride underneath them for their wedding reception. It took several years for the grape vine, under the supervision of one of my cousins, to grow up the wooden structure that I built. Driving past any vineyard you will notice the neat structure built to support the best growth and production of the grape vines. Whether wooden, like my arbor, or a thin metal trellis, the structure is not what produces the fruit. The vine produces fruit, but the structure helps the vine produce healthy and beautiful fruit. When our life is overgrown and lying on the ground, it's difficult to see and taste the fruit. We are smothered and choked by other things and finding that sweet burst of flavor can feel like a random discovery rather than part of who we are. What if we trained ourselves up a structure, like a vine up a trellis, so that our fruit might be healthy and beautiful for everyone to enjoy rather than a secret left to be stumbled upon?

Exercise coaches, trainers, and doctors get this concept when it comes to the fruit of workouts and diets. Think of the structure or trellis as the rhythms of your daily life. Exercising every morning is a rhythm that helps the fruit of your body be healthy and beautiful—exercise is shown to produce healthy chemicals in your body that help you be more creative, productive, and happy. Your strong muscles and great appearance are more of a by product to the real benefits of exercise. Work is a rhythm in your life. The habits and gatherings with family and friends are rhythms—think holidays, traditions, golf outings, regular date nights with your spouse. . .etc. Going to church every Sunday is a rhythm, it does nothing to "save" you. God is not like a school administrator taking attendance and giving you a passing or failing grade—even though as a pastor sometimes I wish it was the case! The purpose of things like weekly attendance at a church for worship is the training and structure it provides. Like the grape vine takes years and constant professional attention to grow up the trellis and remain healthy and beautiful, the rhythms of worship and community found in church are not the fruit but rather the structure our life grows on. This analogy can also be used to see how training our lives up the wrong structure or trellis can lead to fruit that is sour and ugly. One key complaint I hear over and over from parents of teens is that their student is hanging out with "bad" friends. Usually this means the friends are not Christians and do not encourage the teen to keep attending church. There is usually little that I can do in these situations beyond being a faithful presence of Christ, listening, and being supportive. One of the common themes I have observed is that for the most part, teens and children imitate their parents. Most parents would say they want their kids to follow their example but that is often because they are not seriously looking and reflecting on the example they are setting for their kids. By the time children become teens, their rebellion stage is already in full swing—often impacted by what their parents are showing to be their true priorities. While families may have some small rhythm or routine of attending church, the children have picked up more on the subtle (sometimes dominant) rhythms. Whenever I get the chance, I ask parents to reflect on the friendships they have and the people they surround themselves with. You become who you hangout with. You want your kids to produce the fruit of faith? Then structure your life with rhythms that include people of faith and prioritize those in your own life. Are your best friends people of faith?

KNOW: WHAT DO WE KNOW ABOUT GOD? | LIGHTS AND RHYTHMS

Loggerhead turtles come out of the water onto the California beaches to lay their eggs. When the eggs finally hatch, the baby turtles instinctively move toward the ocean, even in the dark cover of the night. For many years, scientists thought the babies were moving toward the sound of the water. That all changed when the young turtles started their mad dash toward the highway that ran along the beach. What they had really been guided by was the light of the moon reflecting off the water. Now, with the lights of the highway, they were confused about what light to use as their guide. We follow the one true light—Jesus. Other things try to outshine Him and take over as our guiding light. . .we need to be able to distinguish between the true and deceptive light, because our role is to point others toward the light of Jesus.[1]

The Apostle John records in chapter 6 that Jesus was out in a remote place on a mountain around the time of the Jewish Passover Feast. This was an annual celebration of the Exodus story that reminded the people of when God freed His people, Israel, from Egypt and they were forced to leave in a great hurry. They were preparing food the night before, and did not have time to put yeast in the bread, so they ate bread made without yeast. The Passover Feast was actually the culmination of a week long celebration called the "Festival of Unleavened Bread". Even in modern day Christianity, we celebrate Communion in our churches. In my heritage, Communion is shared every Sunday; bread without yeast is broken among us as a reminder of God's grace. The Apostle Paul gives a great reason for continuing to use unleavened bread:

> Your boasting is not good. Don't you know that a little yeast works through the whole batch of dough? Get rid of the old yeast that you may be a new batch without yeast—as you really are. For Christ, our Passover lamb, has been sacrificed. Therefore let us keep the Festival, not with the old yeast, the yeast of malice and wickedness, but with the bread without yeast, the bread of sincerity and truth.[2]

During the first days of the Festival of Unleavened Bread, Jewish families go through the whole house and find every last piece of yeast and throw it away. Children do it as a scavenger hunt of sorts and it is a great teaching lesson. The yeast, Paul says, represents our old way of living—the habits of selfishness, darkness, evil, and sin. In communion we are invited to run through our homes, our lives, our hearts and find every last piece of yeast and get it out. A

---

1. Houser. *Building Children's Ministry.* 31–32
2. 1 Corinthians 5:6–8 NIV

little bit of darkness can work through our entire lives just like a little bit of yeast can work its way through a whole batch of dough! Instead we ought to desire our lives to be sincere and full of truth. Perhaps Holy Communion can be a habit forming experience. The next time you taste the cracker—made without yeast—pause for a moment before eating it. Run through your "house"—your life, mind, and heart—what darkness do you need to throw out? Be urgent about it! So that you can be like the bread you are about to eat, unleavened—sincere and true—full of Jesus' light.

Food is a metaphor used over and over by the authors of the four Gospels. Jesus is always eating with people. In John 6 we find Jesus feeding a crowd. Consider the effort and money it takes to get food for so many people. Imagine trying to feed all the students at your nearby middle school. No actually it would be closer to all all the families at that school and the high school and the elementary schools combined. The text tells us that there were 5,000 men. So we can roughly estimate that this number could be doubled or even tripled when you count the amount of women and children that would have also been in the crowd. It's a huge amount of people, where are they supposed to get the food? Jesus turns to his close friends and asks, "okay guys time for a potluck" and they go, "you have got to be kidding. . ." That is my reaction often times. I see the crowd of people—the mission before me, the needs of people, the injustices, brokenness, disasters, poverty, hunger—and get overwhelmed, thinking that I have to provide the food. Jesus explains, "I am the bread of life. Whoever comes to me will never go hungry, and whoever believes in me will never be thirsty."[3] Do not let the enormous crowds—the tasks, dreams, or experiences—overwhelm you, Jesus is the Bread of Life. He is the one who satisfies our hunger with bread that keeps on giving!

Jesus wanted to take care of the people before sending them home, but since creating food out of air was not his style, Jesus worked with what was available. Philip and the disciples found a boy with a lunch: five small flat barley loaves and two dried salty fish. Jesus turned it into enough dinner for everyone. The miracle

3. John 6:35 NIV

demonstrates when we are willing to give even a little, Jesus can bless it and make it go a long, long way! So what are you willing to give Jesus? The light of the World wants to shine on you, shine in you, and shine out of you. Jesus wants to use the small things we trust Him with, to do great things! What small habits are you cultivating now that Jesus may use to multiply in order to feed the thousands?

Nine years ago, Jesus took a small desire in my heart and turned it into something huge in my life. I found myself desiring to host a regional youth retreat to serve our students. This event is still going strong at that church even though it's been five years since I've moved away! I got to be the leader for four amazing years, and I thank God for that. He was able to take a small thing and make a huge life changing moment for me. This one decision has impacted hundreds of lives over the nine years and was really what pushed me to enter ministry full time as a youth pastor. It may seem overwhelming at times, but remember Jesus calming the storm is the very next story following the miraculous feeding. We do not have to fear, or be overwhelmed because Jesus says "it is I; do not be afraid."[4] We too can invite Jesus into our boat when the seas are rough.

The little loggerhead turtles are born with an innate sense to follow the light of the moon into the ocean. It is not hard to see how modern street lights get in the way. Inside all of us are the innate habits of worship and desire for knowing. These are meant to draw us, like the moon draws the turtle, to God. Today, there are so many competing lights (often what Andy Crouch calls vast number of glowing rectangles in our homes—tv's, smart phones, computers, etc) in our world.[5] This is where the rubber meets the road in our lives. The big picture is the concept of our relationship with God: what does knowing God mean? This is important, but it really comes down to our daily habits which are the actual lights in our lives. Every habit becomes a light drawing us toward a destination. When our life is full of habits that light up a freeway full of cars ready to run us over instead of habits that lead to the soothing

4. John 6:20 NIV
5. Crouch. *The Tech-Wise Family.* 131

rhythm of God's vast ocean, we dash towards danger instead of a loving and intimate connection with our Creator. The formation of habits is what illumines our life's trajectory. This is not just a modern problem, but technology and our modern world does bring new faces to the consistent challenge of knowing God.

The Bible tells us that when God rescued the people of Israel from slavery in Egypt, they were in the desert and Moses had an encounter with God. When Moses returned he delivered what has become known as the 10 Commandments.

> [1] And God spoke all these words: [2] "I am the Lord your God, who brought you out of Egypt, out of the land of slavery. [3] "You shall have no other gods before me. [4] "You shall not make for yourself an image in the form of anything in heaven above or on the earth beneath or in the waters below. [5] You shall not bow down to them or worship them; for I, the Lord your God, am a jealous God, punishing the children for the sin of the parents to the third and fourth generation of those who hate me, [6] but showing love to a thousand generations of those who love me and keep my commandments. [7] "You shall not misuse the name of the Lord your God, for the Lord will not hold anyone guiltless who misuses his name. [8] "Remember the Sabbath day by keeping it holy. [9] Six days you shall labor and do all your work, [10] but the seventh day is a sabbath to the Lord your God. On it you shall not do any work, neither you, nor your son or daughter, nor your male or female servant, nor your animals, nor any foreigner residing in your towns. [11] For in six days the Lord made the heavens and the earth, the sea, and all that is in them, but he rested on the seventh day. Therefore the Lord blessed the Sabbath day and made it holy. [12] "Honor your father and your mother, so that you may live long in the land the Lord your God is giving you. [13] "You shall not murder. [14] "You shall not commit adultery. [15] "You shall not steal. [16] "You shall not give false testimony against your neighbor. [17] "You shall not covet your neighbor's house. You shall not covet your neighbor's

wife, or his male or female servant, his ox or donkey, or anything that belongs to your neighbor."[6]

You could call these the 10 rhythms for living with God and others. One way of categorizing them is the first four have to do with our relating to God and the latter six have to do with our relating to each other. As you read through the verses, you might have asked "I don't see Moses giving any numbers, are there really ten?" In fact, some Jewish Rabbis of Jesus' day went through the writings of the Torah and found over six hundred commandments. But these ten have received more attention because, like anything in life, there are priorities. These ten have been prioritized because of the weight and significance they have on the rhythms of life and the shaping of a people. God was bringing the Israelites out of Egypt to become a nation that would live in relationship with God and be what God had intended in the Creation story. Notice how the fourth commandment has an explanation. The Sabbath, the day set apart for rest and worship each week, is rooted in God's own rhythm of creating.

What are your rhythms? All of us have expectations like work, school, maintenance, meal preparation, and relationships that require certain rhythms—some natural and some unnatural (meaning we have to work harder at them). With the invention of the light bulb, work and sleep no longer are mandated by the rising and setting of the sun. An important conversation with those you do life with is regarding the rhythms you prioritize. First, looking at the natural rhythms. Do you eat a meal together once a week and the same time and place? Perhaps your work schedule naturally lends itself to dropping the kids off at school every morning. The unnatural rhythms are a little more difficult. Maybe your parents want to Skype once a week but you can't find a consistent time and often find yourself simply pushing the date. Or perhaps your work doesn't abide by a schedule and you have to navigate that chaos with your partner. Or perhaps your work does not have a consistent schedule which gives you freedom and flexibility but also causes chaos with you and your partner.

6. Exodus 20:1–17 NIV

Christians balk at the idea of Sabbath keeping by invoking Jesus' words "the Sabbath was made for man and not man for the Sabbath."[7] This is true and incredibly freeing from the standpoint of law keeping. But the invitation is to realize what it truly means for the Sabbath to be something made for humanity. It is actually a gift. Rhythms are not meant to be rules and restrictions but rather healthy guard rails and sign posts pointing us to live the way God intended.

I'm sure you've heard someone say, "I need a vacation from my vacation." This is so true! When I think about my recent Christmas vacation, I remember cramming as much as we could into it. Standing in line at Disneyland, wading through crowds, and staying up til all hours of the night talking and playing games. When we come out on the other side of a vacation and back into our hectic lives, we just jump into planning our next vacation! What if we approached it differently? What if, instead of running from one vacation to the next, we practiced God's design for rest.

The Bible refers to this rest from work as "Sabbath." In Exodus 20 verse 8 it is referred to as part of the rhythm of Creation (part of God's great Creative work was rest) and in Deuteronomy 5:12, it is part of the deliverance from slavery in the Exodus story (the people were liberated from slavery and in their freedom God gave them rest). Do not miss this: vacation is not Sabbath because a vacation is not devoted to God. Randy Harris, professor at Abilene Christian University puts it this way: "Sabbath is closely connected to God. . .[and] contains two key elements: playing and praying." You need to learn to play again, to have something completely dominate your entire attention. Do you remember being on the court or in the field, running, and your heart was beating "pass, over here. . .GOAL!" Your mind and body are in unison moving together. God created you to play, but we have allowed ourselves to be reduced to poor multitaskers. The rules regarding the Sabbath were to help people focus on rest and on God. We rest best when our minds and bodies are aligned. We call this play. Play helps us rest in turn enabling our attention to God's presence.

7. Mark 2:27 NIV

God is always near, the trick is to hear. "Mama" Maggie Gobran, a coptic Orthodox Christian lady in Egypt, said this in 2011:

> Silence your body to listen to your words
> Silence your tongue to listen to your thoughts
> Silence your thoughts to listen to your heart beating
> Silence your heart to listen to your spirit
> Silence your spirit to listen to His Spirit
> In Silence you leave the many to be with the One.[8]

Sabbath is so much more than rest from work, it is an opportunity to be with "the One," Creator, Savior, Lord, Almighty, God who gives true rest!

DO: WHAT SHOULD WE TRY TO DO? | RULE OF LIFE

The Rule of St. Benedict would be a great night time reading if you have an over active imagination and need something to put you to sleep. As you read through it, if you get a translation in a language you can understand, you might be a little aghast by the strict nature of it. There are specific instructions for work, prayer, rest, cleaning, worship, and silence. The Rule basically is a training manual for monastic life. We are not all called to monastic life but the monastic rule is really no different than a diet, exercise plan, work schedule, or family calendar. Monks just take the rhythms much more seriously as a spiritual practice. Our desire to know God—to listen in a grounded awareness that is above the static—means we need to remove the overgrowth (see the chapter on *Simplicity*) and train our life up the trellis of a rule of life. Fuller Theological Seminary takes the rule of life so seriously that they have designed four core courses every student in their three schools of Psychology, Theology, and Intercultural Studies have to take. In each course, students are exposed to different spiritual practices surrounding worship, prayer, community, mission, and vocation. The final project for each class is to write a personal rule of life that incorporates practices they have learned. My hope

8. Marshall Shelley, "The Fire Within Mama Maggie," Christianity Today, October 17, 2011, https://www.christianitytoday.com/pastors/2011/fall/mama-maggie.html.

for you is that you will consider looking at your life and reflect on the practices and rhythms you need to form a structure that your life can be trained to grow up and around. Remember the practices (like Bible reading, prayer, going to church, exercise, dieting, sleep. . .etc) are not the fruit of your life or the point. The fruit is what comes from your heart. Things like love, joy, peace, patience, kindness, goodness, gentleness, faithfulness, and self control.[9] The rule of life, or rhythms, are simply there to help you gain the capacity to love deeply and live humbly. Here is an example sketch of my own rule of life as it has developed over the years.

Daily

- Morning Lectio Divina (I use the Pray As You Go App)
- 15 minutes of Centering prayer
- Physical Exercise
- Evening *Gratitude* journal

Weekly

- Hospitality (Inviting others over for Sunday meals)
- Holy High's and Low's with Janel at the dinner table (typically on Saturday night)
- Sabbath on Monday (day with Ashlynn, I avoid being on my phone or computer)
- Friday morning coffee date with Janel
- Sharing stories of life with God in the neighborhood at Wednesday Staff Meeting
- Check-in/Confession with a pastor friend (currently Friday call with Garrett)

9. Galatians 5:22–23 NIV

- Worship—being present (at church and midweek at Fuller Seminary chapel)

Monthly

- Techno sabbath (a day without technology with family, hiking, board games. . .)
- Meeting with either a coach, spiritual director, or therapist (currently a coach)
- Continuous learning: Read a book and listen to a book on Audible
- Track spending each month (use a budget and be aware of how we are doing)

Annually

- Family vacation (where I try to be as tech free as possible)
- Two day silence and solitude retreat to Reassess ROL

Some Thoughts on Practices for Your Rule of Life

My daughter's name is Ashlynn Selah Coburn. The middle name Selah is from the Hebrew for breath, or could be translated pause. This is found in many English translations of the Psalms. The amazing process of having a child does give me pause and takes my breath away—God is good. A practice I suggest you incorporate is breathing. Every year, my aunt and uncle take their family camping (read: glamping) in Central Oregon along the Deschutes River. The fishing has dried up over the years to not be very good, but they still love the campground and the over 40 years of memories they have made going to the same one each year. One year I decided to go all in on fishing and hiking. I spent over eight hours each day hiking up and down the little river several miles in each direction. I am pretty sure I caught only one fish in nearly a week of it all. The time consuming part of the whole endeavor was the meandering way the stream cut through the meadows and the varying flow of the river in the different spots based on things like trees, foliage, and rocks. The fish liked to hide out in certain banks but I was no expert so I probably walked right by a bunch of them. We need to slow down, to pay attention to the meandering flow of our emotions and those around us. I encourage you to look again at the breathing prayer practices I recommended at the end of chapter two in the *Listening Practices*.

Prayer is perhaps the most basic habit in the Christian's life, so we ought to carefully consider how it is forming our knowing of God. Life is lived in community, so no matter how personal you feel your habits of prayer are, they are lights others will be drawn to. Sure, writing a book is pretty cool, but how you start your day and end your day will speak louder to the people closest to you. And the life you live with those closest to you is what will spill over into the ways you influence the world.

Your spouse, family, or roommate, will be drawn into your habits of waking, sleeping, eating. My wife and I's sleeping habits have changed dramatically when she began working full-time as a teacher, and then again when our baby girl was born. I was always a night owl, watching TV or being up until after ten. Midnight was a pretty normal bedtime for me in college and right before we got married. Janel adopted my late night habits when we first got married. But when she started teaching and needed to get up at six o'clock our habits began to shift. She was tired earlier, and her activity in the morning slowly began to invite me to wake earlier too. This happened because we both desired to have the habit of falling asleep together. The problem was I would not fall asleep. In the first two years of our marriage my phone was my alarm and was too easy access and became a distraction to the hard work of quieting my mind to sleep. My TV watching habits involved lots of food too. Snacks, sodas, cheeses, and lots of chocolate milk—made it so my stomach was not ready to lie down. Being used to snacking up until eight or nine o'clock and still having a couple hour buffer to digest, going to bed right at nine after snacking and watching

TV, I physically would toss and turn for hours. Little productive happened in those night time hours. I would stew and spin about the stresses in our life: financial debt, arguments that had been unresolved, drama at work. I would make huge to do lists for my upcoming work week, writing and responding to emails which meant that I never really rested or gave myself space to gain a healthy perspective on all that was happening. We did not even realize how my body and mind carried stresses at night. A more regular rhythm of sleep has helped me notice and address these stresses rather than avoid them and carry them in the dark. Going to bed earlier has led to other shifts in habits too. We have chosen to turn off the TV and put the phones away in our charging station (located in the kitchen, not the bed stand) at eight o'clock. This means most nights we have a full hour to wind down, reflect on our day, talk together, and do our bed time routine. Trying to go to bed right after binging several hours worth of Netflix posed a tremendous problem for me, with an active mind. My wife, exhausted from the long day full of little kids was ready to crash and I would come to bed because that was our habit: fall asleep together.

You see, the simple habit of sleep can actually be a tremendous light shining in your life, is that light distracting for you? It was for me. My wife did not do a theological reflection to identify sleep as a habit I needed to form, instead she formed a habit that helped her and invited me into it. There were many nights she would wrestle with whether or not to ask me to come fall asleep with her. She knew I wasn't always tired, and didn't want to force sleep on me. Sometimes she would ask and other times she wouldn't. Sometimes I needed her to demand I put the email away to form the habit. The journey is not easy and she would be the first to tell you that each night requires many choices—not to watch another episode after eight, not to scroll through Facebook while doing the routine, to really talk and share about the day with each other. The formation of her habit directly impacts me and the habits I form and, as a result, also impact us together. You might not be able to see the trajectory of how your habits will impact others, especially in your church and faith communities, but they will. This is why we need processes for discerning new habits and we need tools and ways of thinking to help with the formation of those habits. This is the tug and pull of individual and communal learning. We learn together about ourselves which in turn changes how we act individually, leading to new ways of being together. I hope the invitation in this book to form *humility, gratitude,* and *simplicity* will forever change the way you are prepared with the loaves and the fish when Jesus calls on you.

Crafting a Rule of Life

One way to structure your rule of life, especially a communal one shared with those you do life with, is to think of a daily, weekly, monthly, and yearly breakdown of rhythms.

- Daily: What practices are key practices we want to shape each day? These may include exercise habits, meals, sleep, TV consumption. . .etc

- Weekly: What practices are important to us as we move through each week? These may include work and time off, church participation, celebrations, free time. . .etc

- Monthly: What frequent practices do we value as we move through the month? These may include techno free days, special outings, service projects. . .etc

- Yearly: What infrequent practices do we want to shape each year? These may include vacations, holidays, life stage transitions like graduations. . .etc

Visual is best. Placing the daily and weekly rhythms in plain sight helps motivate and remind everyone about the rule of life. I would suggest revisiting the rule of life at least once a year but not more than twice. If the rule is in too much of a constant state of flux, it will never truly give life because you will always be adjusting to the new rhythms. But likewise if you do not reflect and adjust the rule of life at least once a year, things once conceived as a good idea can either become stale or simply never really work at all.

Conclusion

Following: Now, Know, Do

NOW: WHAT IS HAPPENING NOW? | LEARNING TO PRAY

Every chapter I have asked three key questions: what is happening now, what do we know about God, and what should we try to do? So what is happening now? Well, you just finished reading a book which means learning is what has been happening. You have been learning specifically about prayer and its relationship to knowing God. This knowing is about more than facts and information; it is an intimate relationship. You learned about three key virtues by following Jesus' example of *humility*, grounding ourselves in a biblical understanding of *gratitude*, and beginning to see our world through a lens of *simplicity*. These three virtues interplay primarily in the basic Christian practice of prayer. "The heart of Christian prayer is getting over the idea that God is somewhere a very, very long way off."[1] This crisis of feeling like God is distant or impossible to know is what I have been trying to address. Prayer is perhaps the central way for us to do this: the Bible teaches us to pray, biblical characters

1. Williams. *Being Christian*. 66

model prayer for us, we learn prayer language and vocabulary from the Christian tradition, and we have our own personal experiences of prayer (both individually and in community). We talk to God and we believe God also talks with us. Approaching prayer as a dialogue, not a monologue, is where the three virtues begin to help us understand and develop a more robust prayer life in which we can glimpse the transcendent and divine life with the Triune Godhead: Father, Son, and Holy Spirit.

Humility teaches us to listen. A relationship cannot be a one sided conversation, we need to quiet our own voice enough to listen. Listening helps us learn to recognize the voice of the other, in this case the great Other we call God. *Gratitude* teaches us be present. A relationship cannot be based solely on the past or the future, we need to recognize God in the present, every day, and ordinary moments of life. *Simplicity* teaches us to see. A relationship cannot have clarity without understanding each other, we need to clear out the noise and interference in order to recognize God's will and plan for our life.

Some of us come with years of praying under our belt, but others may have just begun recently. Some of us are skeptical about the whole practice of closing our eyes and talking aloud to the air. Some of us don't really even think about it, we just do it because we are "supposed to" or have always done it. We should think critically about what prayer is and let that reflection challenge the habits and practices we have. I have submitted that our rhythm of life should involve prayer and we ought to build in various forms of prayer practices: silence, sharing what we are thankful for, and communal prayer. There are lots of ways we can rekindle a dead or dying prayer life with just a few minutes of creativity. We can not let bad prayers become an excuse to let go of this basic and integral Christian practice. But the other side of the coin is also true: sometimes we must be let go of creative and meaningful forms of prayer in order to create space for new practices in different seasons of our life. St. John of the Cross' classic work *The Dark Night of the Soul* has given many the language for how loss and doubt can, in some mysterious way, lead to deeper connection with God. In academic circles this is often referred to as deconstruction. We need to tear down in order to rebuild. The three virtues of humility, *gratitude,* and *simplicity* are my attempt at a reconstructive theology of prayer. My hope is that I have asked some important deconstructing questions about prayer and knowing God which have prompted reflection. My goal has not been to leave us lost and confused but to let Jesus, who came to "seek and save the lost,"[2] reconstruct our prayer life in light of *humility, gratitude,* and *simplicity.*

KNOW: WHAT DO WE KNOW ABOUT GOD? | JESUS ON PRAYER

My favorite question we consider in each chapter is the second one: what do we know about God? I have a huge love for the Bible. I know all the familiar stories and even many of the unfamiliar ones. I love reading the Bible and reading about the Bible. So it makes sense that the primary source for what we know about God, especially what we know about Jesus, comes from it. So when we are learning about prayer and the three virtues, we can follow my childhood pastor's advice and use the Bible as "the straight edge by which we measure how crooked our life is."[3] What we know about God is also found in writings of other Christians, both recently and historically, and in creation. The Bible tells us that creation witnesses and testifies to who God is.[4] So by observing how people act (sociology and psychology) and the way the universe works (science and nature), everything can be an avenue for learning who God is. I love drawing on all these great sources for understanding God and especially understanding prayer. Since my expertise and training is in the Bible and the literature surrounding it, I didn't try to venture too far into the realms of psychology, sociology, or other sciences. Suffice it to say that although my sources are mainly from the Bible, I have total faith that understanding of God can come from a multitude of other places and studies as well. Sometimes we can get lost asking questions about whether a story in the Bible is historically factual like: was Job a real person? I love how Brian

2. Luke 19:10 NIV
3. Pastor Eric Dooley
4. Psalm 19 NIV

Zahnd put it on a podcast I was listening to: "the Bible does one thing perfectly, it points to Jesus."[5] So as we consider what we know about God when it comes to prayer and the interplay of *humility, gratitude,* and *simplicity* let us once again look at Jesus' prayer life.

> [1] One day Jesus was praying in a certain place. When he finished, one of his disciples said to him, "Lord, teach us to pray, just as John taught his disciples."[2] He said to them, "When you pray, say: "'Father, hallowed be your name, your kingdom come. [3] Give us each day our daily bread. [4] Forgive us our sins, for we also forgive everyone who sins against us. And lead us not into temptation."[6]

This is one of the most familiar passages on prayer in the Bible. You may recognize that Luke and Matthew write somewhat different accounts of this event. Rather than a large crowd on a hillside listening to a sermon like is shown in Matthew, Luke says Jesus was off praying. What we know about Jesus is that he did not just teach about prayer, he did it. The disciples come to him to learn to pray because they saw that it mattered to Jesus. Over and over in the gospels we read about Jesus going off to pray.[7] The disciples witnessed the *simplicity* of Jesus' life by how he created margin by going away from the busy and crowded spaces to pray. We marvel at Jesus' obedience to God's will and plan when he dies on the cross, the clarity and understanding of by which he lived out his calling was made possible because of the daily choices he made to pray.

> [1] Be careful not to practice your righteousness in front of others to be seen by them. If you do, you will have no reward from your Father in heaven. . .[5] And when you pray, do not be like the hypocrites, for they love to pray standing in the synagogues and on the street corners to be seen by others. Truly I tell you, they have received their reward in full. [6] But when you pray, go into your room, close the door and pray to your Father, who is

5. Brian Zahnd, "Scripture as Witness," Brian Zahnd (blog), January 1, 2014, https://brianzahnd.com/2014/01/scripture-witness-word-god/.

6. Luke 11:1–4 NIV

7. Matthew 14:23, 26:36; Mark 1:35, 6:46; Luke 3:21, 5:16, 6:12, 9:18, 9:28; John 17:1

unseen. Then your Father, who sees what is done in secret, will reward you. [7] And when you pray, do not keep
on babbling like pagans, for they think they will be heard
because of their many words. [8] Do not be like them, for
your Father knows what you need before you ask him.[8]

This is the precursor instructions to pray the Lord's Prayer. I
have always felt this seemed a bit on the drastic side, but in an age
of social media I have begun to see how easy it is to "pray like the
hypocrites" in public display to get the likes and attention. Jesus
uses secret language to describe our God. Jesus demonstrates that
the God who is in secret is found in secret. This requires a genuine
humility. Jesus is saying that people who put on a good religious
show and pray a lot will not find God. In our discussion of *humility* we centered on listening to God. Jesus packs a punch when he
points out that God already knows what you need long before you
get the gumption to ask for it. This will give us pause the next time
we write a list of things we need to pray about. God already knows
the list and perhaps we are better served listening for what God
wants and knows we need.

This, then, is how you should pray: "Our Father in
heaven, hallowed be your name, [10] your kingdom come,
your will be done, on earth as it is in heaven. [11] Give us
today our daily bread. [12] And forgive us our debts, as we
also have forgiven our debtors. [13] And lead us not into
temptation, but deliver us from the evil one."[9]

Most often when the Lord's Prayer is recited aloud the ending
goes something like "for yours is the kingdom and the power and the
glory forever amen."[10] There are many reasons for this addition and
reasons for why some English translations choose to include or ex-
clude it in the main text of your Bible. As I consider how these words
have shaped my prayer life I realize the message is one of *gratitude* for
God's rule, authority, power, and awesome presence in my life. I am
reminded after making requests for deliverance and protection from

8. Matthew 6:1, 5–8 NIV

9. Matthew 6:9–13 NIV

10. Matthew 6:13 NIV only found in late manuscripts

evil that God is at work in my life, I name those ways by thanking God for them. I thank God in the early mornings for the sunrise and serene beauty of creation, the power of the wind and rain in storms, and the order to the universe I witness. I am thankful for God's awesome creativity, the glory of God, I see in my daughter as she grows and problem solves. I am thankful for the fire fighters who work hard and the government agencies who protect with their God given authority and responsibility to care for us. God has set authorities in place and they remind me to be thankful for God's ultimate authority. Having to list and name these things that I am truly thankful for each week at the dinner table on Saturday night requires a certain perspective and discipline. I am much more conscious of how God is with me when I am practicing prayers of *gratitude* and adding to the joy jar in our living room. So for me even if these words were not uttered from the mouth of Jesus of Nazareth that day on the mount, I believe the Spirit of Christ inspired them and has used them to remind us of the importance of *gratitude.*

DO: WHAT SHOULD WE TRY TO DO? | PRAYING TOGETHER

What now? The third question in each chapter has been the application question: what should we try to do? The underlying assumption with this question is that what we have learned should change the way we behave. So when we think about praying in light of *humility, gratitude,* and *simplicity* modeled by Jesus this should not be left on the pages of a book but lived out in our daily habits. This is why chapter five on rhythms and crafting a rule of life can be so helpful. Taking what we learn and putting it into practice requires hard work and diligence. My wife and I have found we have to talk about something we learned at least four times before we actually begin to put it into practice. Whether it is a new communication technique or prayer practice we are wanting to adopt as a couple, the first several times feel forced and require disciplined intentionality (sometimes we have to physically schedule stuff like our coffee dates on the calendar to make sure it isn't forgotten). Every chapter ended with this practical section trying to draw us into a new imagination of what our life could be like that is in contrast to where we are at now. We want to put into practice what we have learned about prayer.

Jesus was considered a teacher, or in Jewish culture a Rabbi. Rabbi's would have a group of followers—the Bible uses the word disciple. This required a bit more devotion, time, and effort than how many become Instagram, Facebook, and Twitter followers today. Peter, James, John, and the other disciples in the first century couldn't read a tweet to catch up on what Jesus was saying. They couldn't follow from afar, instead it was a messy and difficult journey. The invitation to become Jesus' disciple was costly, "Jesus went out and saw a tax collector by the name of Levi sitting at his tax booth. 'Follow me,' Jesus said to him, and Levi got up, left everything and followed him."[11] Walking around following Jesus meant you were dusty and dirty, without a permanent home or job. The disciples gave up all they had and knew. Following changed their eating and sleeping habits, they had to give up their hobbies and friendships, all to pursue learning from their teacher. With our cars, air planes, microwaves, and fast food restaurants we are very far removed from the patient and time consuming nature of what following Jesus meant for his disciples. We want the quick fix to our relational difficulties and anxieties. We want to read a book and instantly apply it all in our lives. Praying is hard and takes time. Incorporating the virtues of *humility, gratitude,* and *simplicity* into our daily practice will take time. Jesus' friend and follower Peter learned this the hard way. He had three long years to watch Jesus pray. A first row seat to observing his demeanor of *humility.* He witnessed the big and little moments of how Jesus expressed *gratitude.* And how the *simplicity* of Jesus' life helped cut through the noise so that Jesus could truly hear and know God's will. Yet, Peter fell asleep in the garden the night Jesus was betrayed, denied Jesus three times, could not be there at the cross when Jesus died, and returned to fishing afterwards. Peter was in process.

This book is meant to be an introductory handbook for exploring the depths of prayer in light of the three key virtues. Where the rubber meets the road is how you begin to model each virtue in your

11. Luke 5:27–28 NIV

life. As you become the teacher who calls others to follow. We are not meant to do this in isolation. The way we follow Jesus and live with the virtues of *humility, gratitude,* and *simplicity* will impact others. Like the dust Jesus kicked up stuck to the sweaty disciples as they followed close behind, we want our habits and practices of listening, being, and seeing to stick on those following us. Parents, your children are following your example. Adults, young people in your sphere of influence (at churches, schools, and social media) are seeing your example. What might it look like for us to normalize prayer practices that develop an intimate relationship with God? Teens, your siblings and friends are looking to you for what is cool. What if we made prayer cool? Kids, your joy and pure innocence remind us how God intended humankind to be. What would it look like for us to reclaim the pure heartfelt prayer God originally intended?

You may not have someone walk up to you and ask "can you teach me to pray" but how you live your life will teach them. Your *humility* will model for them how to listen for God's voice. Your *gratitude* will ground them in the present and help them be with God who is living and active in their life. Your *simplicity* will help them see God's presence and understand God's will for their life. Don't underestimate your example. Don't let these words remain on the page. Because I love practices, I have adapted a group prayer liturgy (fancy term for the order of a religious service) for you to use with friends, family, or church community. I have laid out some points of intent and then the basic order with some instructions. While it can feel very awkward at first, I highly encourage you to say aloud in unison the written prayer portions. While this liturgy contains written prayers (both from scripture and the Christian tradition) it also offers moments for improvisation and offering your own word in prayer to God.

The Intent of the Prayer Liturgy

- To be attentive to God's invitation to join in with what God is doing in our families, church, neighborhood, city, and world.

- To pray for each other, prayer requests given, and seek God's help.

- To listen to each other and to God through Scripture and communal prayers.

The Liturgy

Bringing Our Attention to God

Spend a predetermined and agreed upon allotted time, usually more than thirty seconds, in silence. Focus on breathing deeply. On the inhale we invite the Spirit of Christ to fill us, and on the exhale we let go of any anxieties, concerns, or distractions. As you become more comfortable the invitation is to extend this period of time longer. A good rule of thumb is start with a stretch goal of two to five minutes and work as a group up to fifteen minutes.

Say Aloud the Jesus Prayer & Lord's Prayer Together

Lord Jesus Christ, Son of God, have mercy on me a sinner.
Our Father in heaven, Hallowed be your name
Your kingdom come and your will be done, On earth as it is in heaven
Give us today our daily bread, And forgive us our debts
as we also have forgiven our debtors, Lead us not into temptation,
but deliver us from evil. For yours is the kingdom and the power
and the glory Forever and ever amen.

God Sightings

Read aloud Psalm 103:1–5
This is an opportunity to center our focus on God by recalling moments of praise and thanks this last week. Have everyone answer this simple question: where have you seen God at in your life this week?

Intercession

- **Prayers for One Another.** In pairs or groups of three share one or two things and spend two to three minutes praying for the other person. Switch off.

- **Prayer Requests.** Gather the requests from Sunday and those turned in via email and as a whole group pray together for each request. This prayer can be led by one person.

- **New Prayer Requests.** Ask for new requests to either be written down, these can be written down and submitted earlier in the evening or announced during this time. Again invite one person to pray for these new requests.

- **Prayers for Our Church Family.** In groups of four or five (or if the whole group is smaller than six) provide three to five minutes to pray for our church. Open it up for anyone to pray as they feel led to for the requests already mentioned, events or ministries, church leaders, and people in our church family.

- **Prayers for Our Community.** In the same groups of four or five provide three to five minutes to pray for our Community. As the transition takes place, there might be something newsworthy to note and encourage people to include in their prayers for the neighborhood, schools, cities, government, and or specific people to pray for. It may also be a time to ask God to bless specific neighbors, or help us become better neighbors.

Listening to God

Listening to God through a Gospel Reading

Re-Orientation Prayers

The Prayer of St. Francis

> Lord, make me an instrument of your peace, where there is hatred, let me sow love; where there is injury, pardon;

where there is doubt, faith; where there is despair, hope; where there is darkness, light; where there is sadness, joy; O Divine Master grant that I may not so much seek to be consoled, as to console; to be understood, as to understand; to be loved, as to love. For it is in giving that we receive. It is in pardoning that we are pardoned. And it is in dying that we are born to eternal life. Amen[12]

Lord, have mercy. Christ, have mercy. Lord, have mercy. Christ has died. Christ is risen. Christ will come again. Lord Jesus Christ, son of God, have mercy on me a sinner.[13]

Continuing the Conversation

My prayer is that this book will be a loaf or fish multiplied in our Creative God's hands. My desire is not that everyone get a master's degree or write a book, but that we all continually reflect on our lives. These sorts of conversations fascinate me, which is why I started a podcast called Value Add: Conversations and Reflections that Add Value to Your Life. The podcast is in many ways a continuation of this book. A way to capture continuous reflection on the formation of our habits and a way to press in with other great thinkers about knowing God in an intimate way. You can follow the podcast by visiting my website, www.valueaddconversations.com or on iTunes by searching in the podcasts section for Value Add Conversations.

Many of the practices in this book have been ones I have tried to incorporate into my life. I would love to hear about other practices of *humility, gratitude,* and *simplicity* you have incorporated into your life. You can reach me on Facebook and Instagram @larscoburn or via email: lars@valueaddconversations.com. I would be

12. Our Catholic Prayers, "The Prayer of St. Francis," n.d, https://www.ourcatholicprayers.com/the-prayer-of-st-francis.html.

13. Inspired by Word of Life Church, "Morning Prayer and Evening Prayer," Liturgies & Devotionals, n.d, http://wolc.com/what-we-do/the-journey-for-adults/worship/liturgies-devotionals/.

honored to hear your stories of reflections on Now, Know, and Do. Let's grab a coffee, I'd love to listen, be with you, and see through your eyes how better to follow Jesus.

BLESSING

I pray your achievements in life and for God will be these:

- You will have fought for what is right and fair.
- You will have risked for what matters most.
- You will have given help to those who were in need.
- You will leave the Earth a better place because of what you have done.
- You will always remember who you are and who you belong to.

> And Now
> May the Lord's Love and Grace be with you, now and for always!
> May you stay blameless until Jesus comes again.
> May you be encouraged and strengthened in every good thing you do and say.
> Know God loves you.
> And through Jesus' grace, he gave you shining hope to continue forever.
> May love and faith be yours from God, the Father, and from our Savior, Jesus Christ.
> May the constant company of the Spirit of God bring you peace beyond understanding.
> And now, to him who is able to keep you from falling
> and present you faultless for the presence of his glory,
> with exceeding joy, glory, majesty, dominion,
> and power, from now to forever more.
> Amen.

Bibliography

Brown, Brené. *The Gifts of Imperfection*. Center City, MN: Hazelden, 2010.

Clark, Chap, ed. *Adoptive Youth Ministry: Integrating Emerging Generations into the Family of Faith. Youth, Family, and Culture*. Grand Rapids, Michigan: Baker Academic, 2016.

Crouch, Andy. *The Tech-Wise Family: Everyday Steps for Putting Technology in Its Proper Place*. Grand Rapids: Baker Books, 2017.

Elwell, Walter A., and Barry J. Beitzel, eds. *Baker Encyclopedia of the Bible*. Grand Rapids, Mich: Baker Book House, 1988.

Emmons, R. A., Froh, J., & Rose, R. "Gratitude." In *Positive Psychological Assessment: A Handbook of Models and Measures*, by M. W. Gallagher & S. J. Lopez (Eds.), 317–32. American Psychological Association, n.d. https://doi.org/10.1037/0000138-020.

Foster, Richard J. *Celebration of Discipline: The Path to Spiritual Growth*. 20th anniversary ed., 3rd ed., Ed. San Francisco: HarperSanFrancisco, 1998.

Hawthorne, Gerald F., David A. Hubbard, Glenn W. Barker, Bruce Manning Metzger, and Gerald F. Hawthorne. *Philippians*. Word Biblical Commentary, [General ed.: David A. Hubbard; Glenn W. Barker. Old Testament ed.: John D. W. Watts. New Testament ed.: Ralph P. Martin] ; Vol. 43. Waco, Tex: Word Books, Publ, 1983.

Houser, Tina. *Building Children's Ministry: A Practical Guide*. Nashville, Tenn: Thomas Nelson, 2008.

Maxwell, John C. "Minute With Maxwell: Who Do You Know That I Should Know?" Youtube, n.d. https://www.youtube.com/watch?v=yZ-leOj9aoE.

McLeod, Saul. "Maslow's Hierarchy of Needs." Simply Psychology, May 21, 2018. https://www.simplypsychology.org/maslow.html.

Moon, Gary W. *Apprenticeship with Jesus: Learning to Live like the Master*. Grand Rapids, Mich: Baker Books, 2009.

Nouwen, Henri J. M. In the Name of Jesus: Reflections on Christian Leadership with Study Guide for Groups and Individuals. New York: Crossroad, 2002.

Porter, Jon. "Egg Picture Beats Kylie Jenner as Most-Liked Instagram Post of All Time." Entertainment. The Verge, January 14, 2019. https://www.theverge.com/2019/1/14/18181806/instagram-most-liked-post-egg-kylie-jenner.

Powell, Kara Eckmann. *Growing Young: Six Essential Strategies to Help Young People Discover and Love Your Church*. Grand Rapids, Michigan: Baker Books, 2016.

Shelley, Marshall. "The Fire Within Mama Maggie." Christianity Today, October 17, 2011. https://www.christianitytoday.com/pastors/2011/fall/mamamaggie.html.

Sivers, Derek. "First Follower: Leadership Lessons from a Dancing Guy." Derek Sivers, February 11, 2010. https://sivers.org/ff.

Ignatian Spirituality. "The Daily Examen," n.d. https://www.ignatianspirituality.com/ignatian-prayer/the-examen/.

Our Catholic Prayers. "The Prayer of St. Francis," n.d. https://www.ourcatholicprayers.com/the-prayer-of-st-francis.html.

Williams, Rowan. *Being Christian: Baptism, Bible, Eucharist, Prayer*. Grand Rapids, Michigan: William B. Eerdmans Publishing Company, 2014.

Word of Life Church. "Morning Prayer and Evening Prayer." Liturgies & Devotionals, n.d. http://wolc.com/what-we-do/the-journey-for-adults/worship/liturgies-devotionals/.

Zahnd, Brian. "Scripture as Witness to the Word of God." Brian Zahnd (blog), January 1, 2014. https://brianzahnd.com/2014/01/scripture-witness-word-god/.

CPSIA information can be obtained
at www.ICGtesting.com
Printed in the USA
FSHW021456090420
69016FS